We estimate a savings of $150,000 in consulting fees alone by using Mr. Jablonski's Approach.

Lima Army Tank Plant

Implementing
Total
Quality
Management

— *Competing in the 1990s*

by Joseph R. Jablonski

Foreword by Paul Hartman

Published by
Technical Management Consortium, Inc.
Albuquerque, New Mexico

Published by:

Technical Management Consortium, Inc.
P.O. Box 13591
Albuquerque, New Mexico 87192-3591
U.S.A.

Library of Congress Catalog Card Number: 90-070518

ISBN 1-878821-00-8

Exhibit 21, Page 81, "Where Is Your Organization in Terms of Quality?", copyright © 1984 by Philip B. Crosby. Survey titled "Profile of a Troubled Company" in reference (Crosby, 1984). Reprinted with permission, McGraw-Hill Book Company.

Exhibit 24, Pages 89 - 93, "Sample Customer Survey," copyright © 1990 by Mackay Envelope Corporation. Prepared by Keller, Rosen and Associates. Survey titled "A Measure of Customer Satisfaction" in reference (Mackay, 1990). Reprinted with permission, Mackay Envelope Corporation.

Special appreciation to

Terry L. Cook, administrative assistance
Donna Fastle, editorial assistance

Third Printing, April, 1992
7 6 5 4 3 2 1
Printed in New Mexico, the United States of America

Dedication

To my wife Patty and sons Joey Jr. and Michael, who stood by my side when I was long on work and short on time.

I love you all

TABLE OF CONTENTS

Foreword

Ford Motor Company, 1974: more than 80% of the automobiles coming off the end of the assembly line go immediately to a rework facility, a factory within a factory. Ford Motor Company, 1978: an ultramodern Ford steel mill is selling steel to small European countries, while Ford buys steel from Japan to get the quality of steel necessary to build cars. Ford Motor Company, 1980: the steel mill closes, turns out the lights and locks the door. Many more Ford Motor Company plants, as well as other auto company plants, will soon follow. All the while, the desks of those trying to administrate the myriad functions of producing automobiles are piled high with paper--mostly multicopy forms, the copies of which most know not where they go nor what their function is.

During those years I started questioning the way we were doing business at Ford Motor. In the mid 1970s I started uncovering evidence that the American automobile industry was not the only business being outcompeted by foreigners. Information on what the Japanese, our offshore competitors (as they are euphemistically referred to in the auto industry), were doing differently was not readily forthcoming from the many top management people I queried at Ford Motor and other businesses.

Researching this mystery, I eventually came upon my first clue: the Japanese designed quality into their vehicles. But what did that mean? We wouldn't know for many years. Our experience, our knowledge, our expertise, and our arrogance would prevent us from knowing. Indeed, it would be many years before we would even recognize the difference between attempting to achieve a deliverable product through inspection, and designing quality into a product and its associated production process (both hard goods and the delivery of services) to achieve quality output.

But some of us, like myself and Joe Jablonski, kept searching and digging. In the early 1980s we were besieged with the Quality Circle panacea to improve quality. Thanks to the concentrated efforts of three gentlemen from Lockheed Aircraft who went to

Japan and, compelled to bring back exciting news of approaches to quality, returned with the most exciting quality improvement concept they observed: let those doing the jobs tell us how we can improve. But the decision makers in this country, those who decided to get on the bandwagon with the other Quality Circle companies, were not listening. They had done their job; they had allowed Quality Circles to be started. Quality Circles were like ships without rudders: those who had the influence to make Quality Circles successful were not at the helm, so the circles drifted aimlessly upon the corporate seas.

The mid 1980s brought the news that the Japanese were using Statistical Process Control (SPC) to identify where things were going wrong. Soon control charts started appearing in abundance. Reports of factory walls being wallpapered with control charts were common. But we didn't know how to use control charts. Nor did we know that SPC involves a wide array of tools other than just those dealing specifically with statistical information. In many cases control charts were used to "check up on" employees, rather than to help the employees understand their processes and how to respond to the information their control charts yielded.

Finally, in the late 1980s, all the tools, concepts, and philosophies of managing for quality started to come together under the name of Total Quality Management, or TQM. We began to understand that none of the aspects of TQM could work by themselves; TQM was a comprehensive management methodology consisting of many facets that had to be applied in a continually changing combination.

Leaders of American business and industry soon learned that in order to orchestrate the implementation of TQM, a change in organizational culture had to be effected. Managers had to stop trying to manage people and learn how to manage people's efforts. They had to stop being bosses and start being leaders. Employees had to get used to the idea that they were no longer expected to "just do the job and don't ask questions"; they were now expected to contribute to improving quality. But how does a corporation change the fundamental facets of its organizational culture?

The way people think about their organization reflects the organizational culture. And people's thoughts affect their actions. Actions, in turn, provide the experience base by which an organizational culture is established. So, to effect changes in an organizational culture, management could work toward changing the way people think, which would, in turn, change the people's actions. This could be a long and arduous endeavor with no method for empirically measuring progress.

On the other hand, management could change its organizational culture by changing the way people do things, e.g., problem prevention by focusing on process improvement, as opposed to problem solving through finger pointing; cooperative teams as opposed to competitive departments. The secret here is that changes in the way we accomplish our organizational missions have to be lead by top management. Jamie Houghton, CEO of Corning Glass, a leader in TQM in this country, says that everybody else in the company is watching him. If he blinks, TQM will flounder at Corning Glass. Top management establishes organizational culture by its actions. Top management establishes the reward system to which people respond; therefore TQM can only be implemented by top management.

Many methodologies for implementing TQM exist, but to my knowledge there is no detailed how-to guide that shows specifically what needs to be done to implement TQM. This book is a guide to show top managers what they need to know and do to implement Total Quality Management.

Joe has personally experienced the failings of business and industry, in both the public and private sectors, resulting from our overall inattention to quality in our processes. Through a discussion of "unquality" and an explanation of one of the best quality metrics, the Malcolm Baldrige National Quality Award, you will gain an appreciation for the many facets of TQM. With an understanding of what TQM is, Joe guides the reader through a phase-by-phase implementation of TQM.

This book describes what all top managers need to know about the facets of TQM: top management involvement, employee involvement, training, process identification and characterization, reward, and supplier quality. A result of Joe's vast experience is his appreciation for the many nuances that can make or break a TQM effort.

While Joe takes a sometimes humorous stand when discussing TQM, his attention to the details of implementing TQM will serve the serious student well. From his prescription for the activities of top management, through the recognition and rewards that will befall Process Action Teams (PATs) as a result of their successful process improvements, to strategies on how to get your suppliers following the same quality approaches, you will learn--Joe will lead you--implementation process by implementation process, to TQM success and a more efficient, more competitive organization.

The phase approach that Joe takes is unique. Step-by-step implementation methodologies become cumbersome when people in an organization don't respond in a lockstep fashion. The phase approach outlined in this book allows phases to overlap, thereby allowing implementation strategies at various organizational levels to be pursued simultaneously.

How top management can use its time and financial resources most effectively is a critical thread that runs throughout the book. You will learn exactly what training is needed for executives and where to get it. Once top executives are trained, Joe describes exactly how to set up what he calls a Corporate Council to make the executive involvement most effective.

While Joe encourages the use of outside consultants, he understands the consulting services can be expensive. Joe teaches the reader when to hire outside consultants, how to find them, when to let them go, and how to get the most for your consultant dollar.

Surveys and research I have done indicate that quality has finally been dragged, albeit kicking and screaming, out of the ''quality department'' in most organizations. We are realizing that quality has to be everybody's responsibility. But how to get everybody aware, concerned, and involved with improving quality? Joe's approach to permeating quality throughout the organization is effective. His guidelines for bringing PATs on line, and having them interact with the Corporate Council assures a TQM implementation strategy that makes quality everybody's business. Moreover, his approach to training PATs does not subscribe to wholesale training. Mass training leaves many people on hold until circumstances allow them to become involved with the TQM effort.

Rather, Joe wisely shows how you can acquire training as it is needed. This makes your training dollar go further because people get to use what they learn immediately, while the application methodology is still fresh in their minds.

The cost of TQM is also covered well. TQM is just like any other improvement to your business. You would expect some period of time to pass before your business realized a return on the investment of a new piece of machinery, a new plant, the addition of a product line, or the training of your management staff in time management. So it is with TQM. The initial investment may seem formidable. But the return on investment is, in most cases, far greater than on any other investment you may make in your company. Not making the investment means, in most cases, that you will be out-competed by someone who does.

And so it is with this book. Here is the Total Quality Management implementation guideline. It is up to you to decide its value to your organization. Every TQM application becomes as much of an individual, with its own identifying characteristics, as individual people are. That is what makes this book all the more valuable as an implementation guide. This prescription is not a lockstep methodology. Rather it is a very flexible, malleable guide, the techniques of which can be applied to any organization whose top executives are serious about implementing Total Quality Management.

Paul Hartman
Manager, Total Quality Management Services
UNC Analytical Services
Albuquerque, New Mexico

Overview

This book's purpose is to offer a road map to implementing Total Quality Management (TQM). It is also intended to aid corporate executives and upper-level managers in their pursuit of increased service and product quality. Those implementing quality management will realize increased productivity, increased customer satisfaction, reduced costs, enhanced quality of worklife, and improved competitive position. However, this book is not for the weak at heart. Rather, it is for those visionaries who realize something important can be gained by implementing Total Quality Management. Sometimes the undertaking will allow a company to achieve greatness in markets that previously seemed stagnant. In other cases, the return may be as simple as allowing a company to compete head-to-head in highly competitive markets, where going out of business had been the only alternative. Regardless of your reasons, if you desire to improve the way you do business, this book will show you how. Happy reading and good luck.

Goal of this Book

The approach this book takes is intended to serve as a strategy for implementing TQM in any company desiring to improve its business practices. Although the specifics of certain factors, such as costs, must be accounted for in tailoring these results to your own company, the underlying assumptions are included to allow the reader to make the necessary adjustments.

This methodology is built on people. The approach recognizes the necessity of obtaining top management commitment, defines what management commitment is, and describes how to propagate that support and enthusiasm throughout the organization. It also recognizes the need for training that is absolutely essential if TQM is to be successfully implemented. The interrelationship of all of the steps necessary to implement TQM is described in detail.

Acknowledgements

I'd like to thank the following people who have helped me in a myriad of ways in the development, preparation, and review of this book.

Content Review

Jon Lund
Janet Modl
Ted Sahd
Patrich Serna

Business Advisement

Mo Shahinpoor Ph.D., P.E.
Walter Yoder Ph.D.

Graphic and Production Support

The University of New Mexico, College of Engineering
The University of New Mexico, Anderson Schools of Business,
Management Development Center

Thank you all.

PAUL HARTMAN

Paul Hartman started learning, teaching, and using Total Quality Management more than 15 years ago as a result of his experiences at Ford Motor Company. Paul left Ford Motor Company in 1980. His efforts were exemplified in the Ford quality movement of the early 1980s.

Paul joined Rockwell International Corporation in 1982. He trained top management in TQM tools and techniques, and he trained and facilitated more than 150 process improvement teams. Corporate functions benefiting from Paul's efforts include procurement, foundry operations, maintenance, word processing, employee benefits, machining operations, payroll, and waste management.

Paul now manages all Total Quality Management (TQM) services at UNC Analytical Services in Albuquerque. He provides TQM Services to government agencies, as well as to business and industry in the private sector. These services include training in all TQM tools, techniques, concepts, and philosophies. Paul also facilitates TQM activities and provides consulting services in TQM. Organizations served by Paul include the United States Department of Energy, Rockwell International, General Electric, EG&G, Inc., departments of the national laboratories, and others.

JOSEPH R. JABLONSKI

Joseph Jablonski is a trainer and consultant on the subjects of Total Quality Management (TQM) and technical project management. He received his B.S. in Mechanical Engineering from the University of New Mexico.

He has experience in technical and financial computer modeling, data processing, testing, manufacturing and project management. He has authored or co-authored more than twenty-five technical and management reports on a variety of subjects.

Joe has successfully implemented TQM in both the private sector and in government. He understands the need to produce better products and services at lower costs to remain competitive in both today's and tomorrow's marketplaces.

Those who have benefited from Joe's training and experience include BDM Corporation, Digital Corporation, General Dynamics, Honeywell, Lima Army Tank Plant, Los Alamos National Laboratories, Northern Michigan Hospital, Sandia National Laboratories, Siemens, Space & Naval Warfare Systems Command, TRW and many others.

Joe is a member of the American Society of Quality Control, the Institute of Industrial Engineers, the National Speakers Association and the American Society of Training and Development. He is also in the 1989 Edition of WHO's WHO IN U.S. EXECUTIVES.

Chapter 1. Introduction

Improving the Way We Do Business

There are many good reasons to improve the way we do business. Our nation no longer maintains its preeminent role as a world producer. Markets once held by the United States are now either gone entirely, or portioned out among our competitors such as Taiwan, China, and others. Of course, we are all aware of Japan's success in automobile manufacturing, semiconductor, and consumer electronics markets. Recent nationwide initiatives such as the Semiconductor Manufacturing Technology Initiative, or SEMATECH (Phillips et al, 1989), have been formed to bolster our ability to compete in expensive technology areas. SEMATECH is a U.S. industry-government coalition whose goal it is to respond to the erosion of American leadership in semiconductor manufacturing technologies. It is an inspiring effort, whose value has yet to be seen, when compared with the intense and focused efforts of the Japanese, to retain that important market they have worked so hard to earn.

Our efforts toward becoming more competitive with foreign products appear to be taking a hold in America. The results of a recent survey of U.S. executives on this subject were described during the National Quality Forum in October 1989. These results indicate that executives believe that as more companies focus on quality improvement, our greatest competitors will come from within our own country and not from overseas. In fact, this trend is expected to continue well into the 21st century. A study by the American Society of Training and Development (ASTD) indicates 57% of all companies surveyed presently have Total Quality as a strategic goal or policy, and the remaining 43% anticipate adopting Total Quality within the next one to three years. In addition, those companies that have begun their Total Quality initiatives have reported satisfactory results in 61% of all cases surveyed. Clearly, those U.S. companies without a Total Quality emphasis now or in the near future will represent a distinct minority--outcasts when compared with the rest of industry. This important initiative is viewed by many as necessary to remain competitive.

One may ask, "I understand the utility of TQM in the manufacturing sector, but what about in service industries?" Marriott Corporation, a service company, is presently implementing the Crosby approach to Total Quality, called the Quality Improvement Process. For starters, employees are now called associates. They are empowered by management to make decisions on the spot rather than having to ask their supervisors. Also more involved in decision making, they are encouraged to do whatever is necessary, within reason, to satisfy the customer.

Other factors come into play in our efforts to become Total Quality Managers. As we move into the 1990s and beyond, the demographics of our nation will change significantly. As a nation, we, ourselves, are competing for a shrinking quality workforce population. The Marriott Corporation, a leader in the hotel services industry, is currently implementing TQM. As a patron of Marriott Hotels, I have always associated the name Marriott with quality, excellence--a company that does things right. Despite Marriott's strong presence in the industry, they are still moving to improve the way they do business and improve the quality of their services to their customers. They view TQM as a means to attract and keep high-quality people to greet customers, maintain facilities, and handle the multitude of tasks and responsibilities necessary to run their hotels smoothly. I could not think of a better example to use in my introductory remarks than Marriott. Their focus on people, both the customer and their employees, is part of their secret to success, the key ingredient that makes things happen. Lastly, their constant enthusiasm for change, to continually improve their operations, is commendable: Marriott equals quality.

TQM: Private and Public Sectors

When thinking of good examples of Total Quality Management, several come to mind. Success in quality in the private sector does not surprise many prospective followers of TQM, but successes in the public sector are often not well known. For that reason, I will cite a good example of each sector.

The private company is Boeing Aerospace Company. Their initiative, Total Quality Improvement (TQI) credits W. Edwards Deming, William E. Conway, J.M. Juran, and Philip B. Crosby for their contributions to the quality profession and for providing the foundation of their effort. Boeing's specific approach relies on extensive research into some quality greats in corporate America such as Armco, Hewlett-Packard, Honeywell Aerospace & Defense, McDonnell Douglas Electronics Company, and others who were willing to share their information and allow Boeing representatives to visit, study, and learn their respective Total Quality initiatives. I am constantly impressed by the quality profession's willingness to share methods so others may succeed. Boeing Aerospace has published an excellent document on their approach and success entitled *Total Quality Involvement - A Resource Guide to Management Involvement*. Although it does not contain the clever remarks or witty humor you will read in my book, it is the most concise document I have read on the ''nuts and bolts'' of problem-solving tools and techniques. These skills will become very important as we move toward Chapter 3 and discuss process improvement. You can obtain your own copy of the Boeing document by writing:

Boeing Aerospace Company
Quality Improvement Center
P.O. Box 3999, MS 85-15
Seattle, WA 98124-2499

Not long ago, corporate leaders believed success stemmed from increasing sales alone. We now realize that if we have a 10 percent profit margin and earn one additional dollar in sales, we will net ten cents additional profit. But, using TQM to reduce costs, we can realize one more additional dollar of profit from saving one dollar in our operations. Admittedly, one dollar of additional profit realized through savings is much better than ten cents of additional profit earned through sales.

As an example of TQM in the public sector, we can consider the City of Santa Ana, which has implemented TQM. Their slogan is "Excellence Through Continuous Improvement." In contrast to the race to improve profits and remain in business in the private sector, the need for TQM in the public sector is different, but no less compelling. In the public sector the challenge is to offer the customer, the taxpayer, an improved quality of services at reduced cost. Santa Ana's pilot project involved seven teams from different departments representing police records, fleet maintenance, building inspection, and others. When someone in the public sector tells me they can't do TQM, I use the City of Santa Ana as a good example. It turns heads. Santa Ana represents a government application of quality to service functions, all of the things that aren't possible to disbelievers. Their teams were trained in much the same manner you will learn about in Chapter 7, and they were successful.

Total Quality Management Defined

Attempts to define TQM have lead to many wandering conversations, meandering trails of misunderstanding and voluminous descriptions. To cut through much of this verbiage and confusion, I would like to offer my own definition of this important term.

TQM is:

> *A cooperative form of doing business that relies on the talents and capabilities of both labor and management to continually improve quality and productivity using teams.*

Joseph R. Jablonski

4

Embodied in this definition are the three ingredients necessary for TQM to flourish in any company: (1) participative management; (2) continuous process improvement; and (3) the use of teams.

Participative management comes about by practicing TQM. Arming your people with the skills and support to better understand how they do business, identifying opportunities for improvement, and making change happen will allow participative management to flourish. Recognizing the capabilities and contributions employees can make to improve business will begin to chip away at the traditional barriers that separate management and labor. This does not happen overnight and will only occur if management listens, and the workforce feels intimately involved with the ownership of the process. Participative management, unlike a light switch, cannot simply be turned on. It is an evolutionary process of trust and feedback which develops over time. Those first few steps toward participative management are slow; it takes time to build momentum. Traditional barriers between management and labor must be breached by that entity willing to take the plunge and offer a show of faith. That is management's responsibility.

Continuous process improvement means accepting small, incremental gains as a step in the right direction toward Total Quality. It recognizes that substantial gains can be achieved by the accumulation of many seemingly unimportant improvements whose synergies yield tremendous gains over the long run. Continuous process improvement reinforces a basic principle of TQM—long-term focus. Corporate leaders must be willing to make an investment in Total Quality today, recognizing that big gains may lie in their future. In fact, the implementation approach described later recommends employees practice their new-found skills on small, achievable victories to improve processes. This approach not only allows the employee to develop confidence in the TQM process, but also provides management with many opportunities to show support and encouragement.

Finally, TQM involves teams. Each team includes a cross-section of members who represent some part of the process under study, from the individuals who work within the process, the suppliers of services and materials brought into the process, and its beneficiaries, the customers. We groom our people to recognize opportunities for improvement within our corporation, understand our business practices, apply a structured approach to problem solving, and offer management recommendations on where to apply scarce resources first, so as to realize the greatest gains. This approach empowers the people directly involved in the day-to-day operations of the corporation to improve their work environment. The employees are aligned with the corporation's goals for improvement. This personal commitment is achieved in exchange for individual and team rewards, recognition, and job security.

Philosophy versus Tools

When speaking to laypeople on the subject of TQM, a picture forms in my mind as to what they think TQM really is. Generally, their perceptions take on one of two forms. First, they may consider it a philosophy of management, or a guiding set of principles that allows someone to manage better. Or they may believe it to be an assortment of sophisticated statistical and measurement tools which few people use in their daily worklife, and even fewer understand. Both points of view are partially correct. There are two distinct elements to TQM—the principles of TQM and the tools.

The philosophy of Total Quality Management allows us to breach the traditional barriers that restrain executives and managers from utilizing the tremendous potential stored in each and every one of their people. This new philosophy emphasizes a few guiding principles and applies to both large and small organizations.

Following the examples of those who have implemented TQM and succeeded, one can better understand how it is possible. The essence of TQM allows us to set our expectations higher than we have in the past, to recognize and remove barriers to change, and to enable high-level managers to solicit the opinions and ideas of their associates and do something with those good ideas. To support the philosophy of TQM we have a set of tools. These qualitative and quantitative tools allow us to better understand the way we do business. They allow us to measure improved quality along the way

6

toward continuous improvement and recognize when we are achieving our goals of improved productivity, performance, efficiency,
worklife, and eventually, improved quality. Many of these tools
have existed for decades, possibly even centuries, but what makes
their use unique today is our recognition that they allow us to focus
on and measure what is important to us. In manufacturing, we can
easily measure a quality parameter, such as fraction of nonconform-
ing product that is discarded prior to customer shipping. In service
companies or administrative functions however, we cannot define
the quality parameter as clearly. Applying these tools to service and
administrative processes allows us to improve the majority of the
work processes around us every day. We recognize quality in this
new environment in reduced customer complaints, reduced reproc-
essing of administrative paperwork, and in some instances, simple
modification of an administrative form to facilitate its use and
reduce data-entry errors. In all cases, whether manufacturing or ad-
ministrative/service applications of TQM, the goal is always the
same: "get it right the first time."

TQM contains an element of time as well. It includes practicing the
tools of TQM to mold individual behavior and imparts a feeling to
the employee that something positive is taking place and progress
is being made. So, in contrast to philosophy driving the organization toward change, the tools oftentimes drive the philosophy at
management and workforce levels within the corporation. As
Schonberger explains, "regardless of the culture, techniques can
mold behavior" (Schonberger, 1986). Yes, before propagating the
philosophy of TQM through the organization, the application of a
few simple tools at the working level can serve to mold behavior.
An example of this technique is how responsibilities previously
reserved for managers are now being handled by regular employees. My wife, an employee of Skaggs Alpha Beta, a grocery store
chain, is now being challenged to take on new responsibilities.
Upon beginning the work day, she graphs sales for the previous day
and provides forecasts of sales into the future. We see several
aspects of TQM at work here. First, she now views the "big
picture," areas previously reserved for managers as if they contained secret or confidential information. She now shares in those

important decision-making responsibilities and can shed light on department forecasts that rely on her intimate understanding of the processes for the past eighteen years. Information such as accounting for holidays, routine peak days in sales, etc., is now generated by the people involved in the process day to day. The strategy not only provides management with better information, but also has the employees "buying into" a certain level of sales, their expectations of how large sales will be. In doing so, employees feel ownership in those projections and will improve service, turn-around time, and all those factors which will make those projections a reality.

This Approach Is Unique

Many approaches have been used to implement corporate-wide change, but this approach is unique because of several aspects in its content and delivery. They are:

1. addressing tough issues and

2. costs and rewards of implementing change

Some of the tough issues I address in this approach include management commitment and resistance to change. Many executives talk about management commitment, but few take on the challenge of describing in detail what they must do to make corporate-wide change, the successful implementation of TQM, a reality. The absence of this important topic in any implementation strategy has time and time again lulled executives into a false sense of security, a belief that they are moving toward TQM when in reality, they are setting themselves up for failure with many adverse consequences to follow. Another tough issue relates to resistance to change. Before agreeing to implement TQM, corporate executives must be aware of resistance-to-change issues and accept the commitment of addressing those inevitable issues before giving the final approval to implement TQM. Ignoring this can postpone a corporate thrust toward TQM and at worst catch corporate executives off-guard enough times so that TQM is scrapped altogether.

Next is the issue of costs and rewards of implementing TQM. The success stories described in Chapter 2 shed light on several of the successful implementations of TQM: those who were undaunted by the challenges of their respective industries, and who rose above the rubble to recapture lost markets amidst tough competition from abroad. Commonly overlooked in these successful corporate transformations are the costs of implementing a corporate-wide quality focus.

I recently had a conversation with a member of the government's Senior Executive Service (SES) on implementation in his organization. Although not an expert on the subject, he had taken several introductory courses in TQM. As I went through my outline of how TQM is implemented, he stopped me when I came to the section on Resources. He exclaimed, "What's this? I thought quality was free," a popular term first used by Philip Crosby, a guru in the U.S. quality movement (Crosby, 1984). I then explained that quality is better than free, you can make money on it, but there is a cash flow problem. Like the student attending classes at a local university, the executive makes the commitment of time and money so he may reap the rewards of that investment in the future. The student's return on investment for a college degree may be a better job at higher wages or greater prestige. The rewards for implementing TQM are reduced costs (as the quality focus becomes part of your day-to-day manner of doing business), increased customer retention, improved employee pride in workmanship and increased market share. Quality is better than free, you can make money on it. But you, as a corporate leader, must be willing to make the up-front commitment of time and money.

> *Quality is better than free, you can make money on it, but there is a cash flow problem.*
>
> Joseph R. Jablonski

Challenge of Change

You may be asking yourself, "If there is an investment of time and money involved with implementing TQM, why bother?" This is a good question. The decision to implement TQM is frequently based on two reasons, neither of which require an in-depth economic analysis. The two basic reasons that present CEOs "take the plunge" are (1) they recognize that there is something to be gained, or (2) they have no choice.

The first category of CEO is the visionary. He may have just returned from a professional conference, reviewed a trade publication, or been prompted by a competitor's improved position in an area that had previously been reserved for your company alone. Whatever the reason, as a special leader, he recognizes TQM as the mechanism where he can now recapture lost ground, revive old markets, and create new ones. The executive sees TQM as an opportunity that doesn't require in-depth cost justifications or a myriad of subordinate presentations. If you decide you fall into this category, you should be applauded, because you represent one of the chosen few. With a minimum of information, you take on the important challenges of corporate-wide change on the feeling, the faith, that your company will benefit.

Everyone else changes the way he does business because he has to. Sometimes valued customers with enough leverage to compel an executive to change may have already been bitten by the TQM bug and realize the power in this new initiative. One of the most inspiring examples of this situation is the Motorola Corp. They made a tough decision that has become the focus of much debate. They require all of their suppliers eligible for the Malcomb Baldrige Award to sign a statement as to their intent to compete. They are, in fact, challenging their suppliers to take on tough new standards and compete head-to-head for the most prestigious of quality awards in this country (Dept. of Commerce, 1990). In exchange for this commitment, their suppliers become part of a winning team with proven success. I believe Motorola's leadership-by-example initiative is a good example to follow.

In another instance, companies may decide to implement TQM because they have gotten so bad at what they do, they feel there is no choice. In this case, an analogy can be drawn between a troubled company and an alcoholic. Like the corporate executive, the alcoholic suddenly realizes that in order to survive and eventually prosper, he must change his ways. Anything short of revolutionary change is inadequate and will eventually lead him back to his old, bad habits. Unlike the alcoholic, the corporation can remove any resemblance of permanent biological damage that might be associated with the company's old way of doing business. Like an alcoholic, the corporation must continually be reformed, the newfound focus toward quality restated again and again, and an aggressive personalized plan for self-improvement adopted.

Not everyone in industry has the luxury of deciding whether or not he will implement TQM in his business. Everyone, consciously or unconsciously, recognizes he is making important decisions today that will either insure a competitive posture into the next century, or place the final nail in the coffin.

Problem Company: Tell-Tale Signs

It has been said "ignorance is bliss." This is true, at least in the short term. I once heard the following story about a perception of quality. "On the first of every month, quality was king. Management spoke of quality and encouraged improvement of quality. Defective products and services were nipped in the bud and corrected prior to ever making it into the hands of the customer. But, as the first of the month passed and the middle of the month approached, quality took on a new meaning. As the end of the month came closer, the motto became 'ship it and we'll fix it in the field,' or 'we'll accept it as a return later. But for now, we can book the shipment and look good on paper.'"

Ignorance is bliss and is reflected in the short-sighted type of management just described. Management often does not recognize the problems with the way they conduct business, or they would surely change their ways. For that reason, I elected to include this section in my book so that management might better understand the "tell-tale signs of un-quality."

This understanding of un-quality was first brought to my attention by a young woman who noticed two key points that had eluded me in my own experience on this important subject. First, she recognized certain things one could notice, or better yet look for, that would suggest the need for improvement. Second, and most important, she observed a cyclic behavior to un-quality; it feeds on itself. In sharp contrast to TQM, where you are continually moving to improve the way you do business, un-quality continually degrades quality, productivity, and most importantly, employee morale.

The signs of un-quality are displayed in Exhibit 1. A department, division, or entire organization may enter this cycle at any point. Let us say, the quality of goods and services in a company decreases. The reason at this point is unimportant. We notice the time necessary to accomplish this process increases. This may be the result of conflict between personnel, unclear procedures, or any number of reasons. Usually as a reflex response, management increases the number of inspections. This makes sense under the traditional way of doing business. Employees can't be trusted to "do it right the first time"; therefore, we will "inspect quality in." As a result, morale suffers and workers--often the better employees--begin to leave. The number of management meetings increases to discuss this growing problem, finger-pointing flourishes, the phone rings constantly with customer complaints. Management concludes these problems are obviously the fault of the workers; therefore, they respond by managing the work force more, not better (AKA micro-management). We have now come full circle, and because of the accumulation of bad management decisions, we witness further quality deterioration. The cycle goes on and on.

The sequence of events may differ from company to company, but the outcome remains the same. Early on, the effects of reduced quality are hidden from management by shipping poor quality goods or providing inadequate services. The books look good because quotas are made, but the hidden problems resurface elsewhere later, usually for an increased cost. Your best employees have left and it is difficult to hire the better prospects off the street because you have a bad reputation. Field returns rise, and you find yourself fixing problems at about 100 times the amount it would have cost to correct them in the plant or prevented in the first place.

Last, and most important, morale has deteriorated and the traditional barriers between management and labor are further reinforced, because the workforce was blamed before the cause of the problem was even understood. Poor credibility between management and labor was reinforced because quality standards were

12

EXHIBIT 1.

Signs of Un-Quality

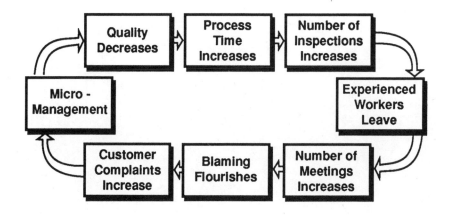

conveyed as a variable. Products and services of unacceptable quality on the first of the month were shipped on the 30th regardless. To the employees, there were no standards to follow.

I could go on describing how the cycle continues, eventually resulting in lost sales and lost jobs, but that is not the point. The important point is that management can recognize tell-tale signs and identify opportunities for improvement. If you can relate to any of my comments above, I will have been half-successful by merely getting you thinking. If you go one step further and say you are going to do something about your company's problems and TQM is your vehicle to success, we will both succeed.

Chapter 2. A Standard of
Excellence

Malcolm Baldrige National Quality Award

When first considering a quality focus, corporate executives wrestle with the question, "What is the 'measuring stick' for quality?" While the specific answer varies from company to company, an excellent starting point is the examination criteria for the Malcolm Baldrige National Quality Award.

The Malcolm Baldrige National Quality Improvement Act of 1987, Public Law 100-107, signed by President Reagan on August 20, 1987, establishes an annual United States National Quality Award. The purposes of the Award are to promote quality awareness, to recognize quality achievements of U.S. companies, and to publicize successful quality strategies.

The Award formally recognizes companies that attain preeminent quality leadership and permits these companies to publicize and advertise their awards. It encourages other companies to improve their quality management practices in order to compete more effectively for future awards. It develops and publishes Award criteria that will also serve as quality improvement guidelines for use by U.S. companies. Furthermore, it widely disseminates non-proprietary information about the quality strategies of the Award recipients. It gets the word out that quality is achievable.

Up to two Awards may be given each year in each of three categories: (1) manufacturing companies or subsidiaries; (2) service companies or subsidiaries; and (3) small businesses. Fewer than two Awards may be given in a category if the high standards of the Award Program are not met. Businesses incorporated and located in the United States may apply for the Award. Subsidiaries--divisions or business units of larger companies--are eligible if they primarily serve either the public or businesses other than the parent company. For companies engaged in both services and manufacturing, the larger percentage of sales determines the classification. For purposes of the Award, small businesses are defined as independently-owned businesses with not more than 500 full-time employees.

Application Process

The application consists of: (1) an Application Form providing basic information about the company; (2) a Site Listing and Descriptors Form providing information about the company's locations and functions performed; and, (3) an Application Report addressing a set of 44 examination items.

A Board of Examiners reviews and evaluates all applications. Comprised of more than 100 quality experts selected from industry, professional and trade organizations, and universities, the board meets the highest standards of qualification and peer recognition. Examiners take part in a preparation course based upon the examination items, the scoring criteria, and the examination process.

Examination Process

The Malcolm Baldrige National Quality Award Examination applies to manufacturing and service businesses of any size. The examination permits evaluation of the strengths and areas for improvement in the applicant's quality systems and their results. It addresses all aspects of quality improvement results using the following seven evaluation categories:

1.0 Leadership

2.0 Information and Analysis

3.0 Strategic Quality Planning

4.0 Human Resource Utilization

5.0 Quality Assurance of Products and Services

6.0 Quality Results

7.0 Customer Satisfaction

Each category is assigned a number of points totaling up to 1,000. Exhibit 2 shows the examination categories, along with the point allocations. It's not surprising that Category 7.0, Customer Satisfaction, carries the most weight in the examination process (300 points). Its nearest competitors, Human Resource Utilization, Quality Assurance of Products and Services, and Quality Results, each carry 150 points.

The Leadership category examines how the senior executives create and sustain a clear and visible quality value system, along with a supporting management system, to guide all activities of the company toward quality and excellence. Examiners also consider senior executives' and the company's quality leadership and support of quality developments, both inside and outside the company.

The Information and Analysis category examines the scope, validity, use, and management of data and information that underlie the company's total quality system. This category also examines the adequacy of the data and information to support a prevention-based approach to quality based upon "management by fact."

The Strategic Quality Planning category examines the company's planning process for retaining or achieving quality leadership and the company's integration of quality improvement planning into the overall business planning. It includes the company's priorities to achieve and/or sustain a quality leadership position.

The Human Resource Utilization category examines the effectiveness of the company's efforts to develop and utilize the full potential of the workforce for quality—including management—and to maintain an environment conducive to full participation, continuous improvement, and personal and organizational growth.

EXHIBIT 2.

Malcolm Baldrige National Quality Award Examination Categories, Items and Point Values

1990 Examination Categories		Maximum Points
1.0 Leadership		100
1.1 Senior Executive Leadership	30	
1.2 Quality Values	20	
1.3 Management for Quality	30	
1.4 Public Responsibility	20	
2.0 Information and Analysis		60
2.1 Scope and Management of Quality Data and Information	35	
2.2 Analysis of Quality Data and Information	25	
3.0 Strategic Quality Planning		90
3.1 Strategic Quality Planning Process	40	
3.2 Quality Leadership	25	
3.3 Quality Priorities	25	
4.0 Human Resources		150
4.1 Human Resource Management	30	
4.2 Employee Involvement	40	
4.3 Quality Education and Training	40	
4.4 Employee Recognition and Performance Measurement	20	
4.5 Employee Well-Being and Morale	20	
5.0 Quality Assurance of Products and Services		150
5.1 Design and Introduction of Quality Products and Services	30	
5.2 Process and Quality Control	25	
5.3 Continuous Improvement of Processes, Products and Services	25	
5.4 Quality Assessment	15	
5.5 Documentation	10	
5.6 Quality Assurance, Quality Assessment and Quality Improvement of Support Services and Business Processes	25	
5.7 Quality Assurance, Quality Assessment and Quality Improvement of Suppliers	20	
6.0 Quality Results		150
6.1 Quality of Products and Services	50	
6.2 Comparison of Quality Results	35	
6.3 Business Process, Operational and Support Service Quality Improvement	35	
6.4 Supplier Quality Improvement	30	
7.0 Customer Satisfaction		300
7.1 Knowledge of Customer Requirements and Expectations	50	
7.2 Customer Relationship Management	30	
7.3 Customer Service Standards	20	
7.4 Commitment to Customers	20	
7.5 Complaint Resolution for Quality Improvement	30	
7.6 Customer Satisfaction Determination	50	
7.7 Customer Satisfaction Results	50	
7.8 Customer Satisfaction Comparison	50	
Total Points		**1000**

Source: Dept. of Commerce

The Quality Assurance of Products and Services category evaluates the company's systematic approaches for total quality control of goods and services, based primarily upon process design and control, including control of procured materials, parts, and services. This includes the integration of quality control with continuous quality improvement.

The Quality Results category examines quality levels and quality improvement, using objective measures derived from analysis of customer requirements and expectations and from analysis of business operations. This category also considers current quality levels in relation to those of competing firms.

The Customer Satisfaction category evaluates the company's knowledge of the customer, overall customer service systems, responsiveness, and ability to meet requirements and expectations. This category also examines current levels and trends in customer satisfaction.

Site Visits

At least four members of the Board of Examiners review each application. High-scoring applicants are selected for site visits, made by one or more teams of examiners. A panel of nine judges from the Board of Examiners reviews all data and information and recommends Award recipients. Award recommendations are based not only upon scores applicants receive on the written examination, but also upon the judges' assessment of overall strengths and areas for improvement as determined from site visits. The recommendations of the judges are final and not subject to appeal. All applicants receive written feedback, summarizing strengths and areas for improvement relative to the Award examination categories.

The highest scoring candidates for the Award undergo site visits by members of the Board of Examiners. The primary objectives of the site visits are to verify the information provided in the Application Report and to clarify issues and questions raised during review of the Report. The candidates receive a site visit agenda at least two weeks prior to the visit. The site visit agenda includes, but is not limited to, a schedule of planned visits to the applicant's facilities and operating units, a list of corporate officials to be interviewed, an estimate of time requirements for the visits, and the names of examiners scheduled to participate. During site visits, applicants make presentations, and examiner teams conduct interviews and review data and pertinent records. The number of examiner team members and the time required for site visits varies according to the complexity of the Award application and the number of sites to be visited. Sampling methods and recommendations from the examiners help determine the number of sites visited. Most visits last two to three days. Site visit teams prepare reports for submission to the judges. During site visits, applicants may be asked to provide data for inclusion in this report. Additional information or data will not be accepted from the applicant once site visits are completed, unless specifically requested by the Board of Examiners. Applicants selected for site visits will be asked to authorize review of their tax status regarding filing of tax returns, payment of taxes, and absence of criminal offenses and fraud. The information ensures suitability of the applicant as a national Award winner.

Confidentiality

All applications are treated confidentially. Applicants do not provide or reveal proprietary information regarding products, processes, or services. Examiners are assigned in such a way as to avoid conflicts of interest. All Examiners sign nondisclosure agreements. Information regarding successful strategies of Award recipients may be released only after receiving written approval from recipients.

Awards

Awards are presented each year in November. Award recipients receive a medal contained in a crystal base. The medal bears the inscriptions, "Malcolm Baldrige National Quality Award" and "The Quest for Excellence." Recipients may publicize and advertise receipt of their Award, provided they agree to share information about their successful quality strategies with other American organizations.

Those Who Succeed

On November 2, 1989 President Bush and Secretary of Commerce Mosbacher presented the Malcolm Baldrige National Quality Award to two companies--Xerox Corporation's Business Products and Systems, and Milliken & Company. These two companies were chosen from among forty applicants amidst stiff competition.

Xerox Business Products and Systems

For the first fifteen years, Xerox was without equal, best in the industry whose products were synonymous with its name. But in the mid-1970s challenges came from foreign and U.S. competitors, as they surpassed Xerox reprographic products in both cost and quality.

No longer even second best in some product categories, Xerox launched an ambitious quality improvement program in 1984, to arrest its decline in the world market it had created. Today, the company can once again claim the title as the industry's best in nearly all copier-product markets. As a result, Xerox not only halted loss of world market share, but also reversed it.

Xerox introduced the world's first plain-paper copier in 1959 and to this day remains the largest provider of copiers and electronic printers. Xerox produces nearly 30 percent of the more than four million copiers in the United States.

Xerox Business Products and Systems (BP&S), headquartered in Stamford, Connecticut, attributes the turnaround to its strategy of "Leadership Through Quality." The company defines quality through the eyes of the customer, perhaps more so than any other company, both inside and outside the copier industry. Xerox BP&S knows what customers want in products and services.

Directed by CEO David T. Kerns and his senior management team, the Leadership Through Quality thrust has made quality improvement and, ultimately, customer satisfaction the job of every employee. All have received at least 27 hours of training in problem-solving and quality-improvement techniques. The company has invested more than four million man-hours and $125 million in educating employees about quality principles.

Xerox workers are vested with authority over day-to-day decisions. And they are expected to take the initiative to identify and correct problems that affect the quality of their products or services. Both salaried and hourly personnel have embraced these added responsibilities.

For example, the company's 1989 labor contract with the Amalgamated Clothing and Textile Workers' Union pledges employee support to "continuous quality improvement while reducing quality costs through teamwork and the tools and processes of Leadership Through Quality." This partnership with the union serves as a model for other corporations.

Customers have noticed the improvements. According to Xerox surveys in 1984, competitors' machines ranked highest in customer satisfaction in all six product categories. Today, Xerox copiers top five of the six categories in Xerox surveys and rank similarly in industry surveys. Not coincidentally, the increase in customer satisfaction parallels the company's gain in world market share over the same span.

The thrust of Leadership Through Quality is ongoing with Xerox BP&S. The process of continuous quality improvement, directed toward greater customer satisfaction and enhanced business performance, is currently targeting a 50-percent reduction in unit manufacturing cost and four-fold improvement in reliability by 1993. Such goals illustrate the commitment contained in the Xerox Quality Policy, "Quality is the basic business principle at Xerox."

Milliken & Company

Ten years ago, Milliken, a major textile manufacturer long recognized for quality products and the use of state-of-the-art technology, asked why some Japanese competitors achieved higher quality, less waste, greater productivity, and fewer customer complaints while using less advanced technology than Milliken's. The reasons, company executives found, lay in management approaches and in personnel practices that, along with technology, drive improvements in quality and efficiency.

In 1981, senior management set in motion Milliken's Pursuit of

22

Excellence (POE), a commitment to customer satisfaction that pervades all levels at all locations. The impressive results improved what had already been an enviable record of quality and performance. In independently conducted surveys, Milliken tops the competition in all 15 measures of customer satisfaction.

Commitment to quality and customer satisfaction begin at the company's highest level, with Roger Milliken, chief executive officer, and Thomas J. Malone, chief operating officer, devoting more than half their time to Milliken's POE process.

Through the Policy Committee and Quality Council, top management creates the environment and provides the leadership for quality improvement, closely monitoring the progress of each company unit toward quality goals.

The approach works so well that Milliken has reduced the number of management positions by nearly 700 since 1981, freeing a large portion of the workforce for assignment as process improvement specialists. The ratio of production to management associates has increased by 77 percent.

Teams are the hallmark of what observers now call the Milliken Quality Process. In 1988, 1,600 Corrective Action Teams were formed to address specific manufacturing or other internal business challenges, and about 200 Supplier Action Teams worked to improve Milliken's relationship with its suppliers. In addition, nearly 500 Customer Action Teams were formed to respond to the needs and aims of customers, including development of new products. Beyond demonstrating a commitment to customer satisfaction, these teams have created marketing opportunities that generate substantial additional sales revenue.

Complementing its many activities to extend the capabilities of its workforce, Milliken invests heavily in training. The company spent about $1,300 per associate in 1988. Training also extends to Milliken's suppliers and customers. Each year since 1984, more than 7,500 visitors have received training in quality principles at Milliken's dedicated training facility.

Suppliers play an important role in Milliken's quality success.

Through extensive efforts in developing supplier partnerships, the company has reduced the number of its suppliers by 72 percent since 1981.

Milliken also maintains extensive databases on environmental and safety variables, suppliers, and customers, including the results of extensive annual surveys on customer satisfaction. In addition, the company "benchmarks" the products and services of about 400 competitors, providing concrete measures for assessing performance and identifying marketing opportunities. Through this surveillance, Milliken determined, for example, that it trailed some competitors in meeting delivery targets. As a result, Milliken improved its record for on-time delivery from 75 percent in 1984, to an industry best of 99 percent in 1988.

The company intends to achieve a ten-fold improvement in key, customer-focused quality measures over the next four years. Each advance brings this innovative company closer to its long-range goal of a production system that fully responds to customer needs, providing, as Milliken says, "products that customers want, in the quantity they want, when they want them" (Stratton, 1989).

Closing Remarks

> *Quality is the key to making American products. We are in the midst of a technological revolution, and our work to build quality products will be a crucial link to the long-term success of the United States in the global marketplace.* (Dept. of Commerce, 1990).
>
> George Bush

For more information on the Malcolm Baldrige National Quality Award, call or write:

> Malcolm Baldrige National Quality Award
> National Institute of Standards and Technology
> Bldg. 101, Room A537
> Gaithersburg, Maryland 20899
> (301) 975-2036

Chapter 3. TQM Implementation

At the conclusion of Chapter 1, I described the tell-tale signs of Un-quality. Let us now focus our attention on those positive characteristics that will allow you to implement TQM in your company successfully. I call these attributes the principles of Total Quality Management.

The Six Principles of TQM

TQM involves six basic principles: (1) customer focus, (2) focus on the process as well as the results, (3) prevention versus inspection, (4) mobilizing expertise of the work force, (5) fact-based decision making, and (6) feedback (see Exhibit 3). Each is described in detail below.

(1) A Customer Focus - All of us recognize that our time on the job is spent performing tasks that will somehow support a sale. We, as a corporation, are in business to provide goods and services in exchange for revenue. Although this concept is neither new nor surprising to us, we must regularly reinforce it at all levels within our organization. As we move toward TQM, we acknowledge the existence of many customers we may have overlooked in the past. This includes the customer outside an organization, who places orders with us. I refer to this customer as the big "C." In addition, there is a little "c," the customers within our company whom we work with on a daily basis. Little "c's" include visual aide support

support from graphics, payroll processing bi-weekly employee checks, finance generating advances for corporate travelers, etc. We relate well to the big ''C'' but our support and enthusiasm oftentimes wane when we support the little ''c's.'' This frequently results from our indirect compensation for these services. Because we do not exchange funds for these internal services, it is difficult to draw a connection between the services the little ''c'' provides and the revenue it receives. As we implement TQM, we shift to a heightened awareness of all our customers, both the big ''C'' and the little ''c.''

EXHIBIT 3.
Principles of TQM

1. A Customer Focus

2. A Focus on Process as Well as the Results

3. Prevention versus Inspection

4. Mobilize Expertise of Workforce

5. Fact-Based Decision Making

6. Feedback

© Joseph R. Jablonski, 1990

I remember one instance when I stopped by the graphics department to drop off some charts for a presentation scheduled in the near future. While discussing my requirements, chart by chart, the graphic artist continually nodded his head in agreement. We were in sync, or so I thought. I then proceeded to ask, ''When can I have the completed charts?'' to which he replied, ''Two weeks is our normal turn around time.'' I said that's OK. He then went on to say,

26

"of course that's unless we get bogged down in our ongoing work, or unless we get a higher priority job."

Dumbfounded, I repeated myself—something I don't usually do. I said, "When can I have my charts?" He made no promises. "No problem", I said, "I will take my work where I know it will be done when I need it." I then gave the work to an outside firm which did a fantastic job and met my schedule. They also charged me a lot of money. But that wasn't much of a concern at the time. I expected to derive millions in work from this presentation and considered the amount an investment—a good investment as it turned out. The moral of the story is that people in need go to whatever source they require to get the job done. Oftentimes cost is not a big issue; their "quality parameter" is measured in turnaround time. They want a certain kind of presentation, a "picture to convey their point." They seek quality, and if the organization itself is not willing to meet the customers' expectations, they will go elsewhere.

(2) A Focus on the Process as Well as the Results - We are the customer for goods and services both from within and outside our company. When we receive a product that does not meet or exceed our expectations, we traditionally go to a competitor or complain, if we think it might get results. Under TQM, we use these deficient results, or un-met expectations, as symptoms—indicators that something is amiss with the process that produced them. Later in the second phase of this implementation methodology (Chapter 6), we will see how these symptoms result in action to correct these deficiencies and continually move to improve the quality of goods and services, using a structured approach to problem solving.

(3) Prevention versus Inspection - Having placed attention on the process as well as the results in Principle #2, the application of Principle #3, Prevention versus Inspection, becomes readily achievable. Before TQM, management believed they could inspect quality in. When something went wrong in the production of goods and services, as a knee-jerk reaction they provided more inspectors. Not so with TQM. Here we apply a structured approach to problem solving and make the necessary investment to understand the process and sources of process variation. We then provide the necessary process controls to ensure every product and service meets an acceptable, predictable quality. TQM Principle #3 directs attention toward the prevention of defective products and services, rather than discovering defects and deficiencies after resources have been spent.

(4) Mobilizing Expertise of the Workforce - A traditional management atmosphere assumes the workforce consists of mind-less individuals wanting nothing more than a pay check. TQM changes this manner of thinking profoundly. First, we recognize that we can compensate individuals for their efforts in many ways; financial compensation is only one method. Studies have shown that individuals hire on and stay with a corporation for various reasons. The salary or wage is not the only reason, nor is it first and foremost. People like to feel appreciated, and TQM creates new, innovative ways to recognize individuals for their efforts. Second, your workforce represents a tremendous wealth of knowledge and opportunity to improve the way you do business, increase profits, reduce costs, and make employees feel as if they are part of a team-- a winning team. A movement toward TQM mobilizes the expertise of the workforce in a very positive way for the mutual benefit of everyone involved.

(5) Fact-Based Decision Making - An Un-quality organization relies on finger-pointing and blame to shift responsibility for unsuc-cessful deeds. A Total Quality organization applies a structured approach to problem solving as ''opportunities to improve.'' The ''TQM approach'' recognizes everyone involved in the process including executive, management, workforce, and customers, and acknowledges that they can contribute to a mutually-beneficial solution. It means understanding the process you work in and around everyday, understanding the cause of your problems, and gathering information, data on which you can base decisions for improving that process. It relies heavily on excellent team-build-ing, communications, and interpersonal skills to develop and yield the best your people can offer. Personality conflicts and personal biases are overcome with one common focus--process improve-ment with everyone lending a helping hand and no one being blamed.

(6) Feedback - The sixth and final principle of TQM is feedback. This one principle allows the other five principles of TQM to flourish. Here, communications is key. To an engineer, it would be unthinkable to design hardware without some element of feedback. For an automobile going down the highway, feedback may be as simple as an speedometer indicating the speed at which the vehicle is traveling. For a spacecraft traveling through space, unaided by man for instantaneous decision-making processes, feedback comes through an assortment of sensors which allow it to make decisions on its own. In manufacturing, feedback may take the form of a graph that flags the operator so a tool can be changed out, preventing production of an out-of-tolerance part. In an administrative function, feedback may take the form of a supervisor sitting next to a valued employee reviewing his annual evaluation. This one-on-one, or person-to-person, feedback is probably the most important, but seemingly the most difficult for line supervisors to accomplish. A technique I have used in providing such feedback is called "three-in-one," like the oil. Offer your employee three portions of encouragement, positive reinforcement and support along with one pointer to grow on. For example, while reviewing an annual evaluation with Fred, your comments may go something like this:

"Fred, I've evaluated you based upon my observations of your performance over this past year. Of course, I based my evaluation on the standards we both agreed upon one year ago. I would like to begin by saying you have these distinct strengths. They are (1)_____, (2) _____,(3) _____. One area where you were satisfactorily evaluated, but have an opportunity for continuous improvement is _____. This is how I can help _____."

The greatest responsibility for a supervisor comes about not from managing money, facilities, or schedules, but rather by leading people to grow. That is the greatest challenge of supervising, and providing honest feedback, with an obvious, sincere desire to help your people grow, will make you the employer of choice.

It should be noted that in many respects, TQM is nothing more than a reemphasis of basic personnel management practices. Working with employees one-on-one to develop performance goals, feedback (hopefully more than once a year), and encouragement are fundamental to those skills that allow managers to successfully climb the corporate ladder. At the foundation of all these skills is the ability to lead, to get people to do what they ordinarily would not have done voluntarily on their own. But they do it because you lead them in a manner that inspires them to be creative and to take a chance. They view you as fair, as someone who will acknowledge their efforts and their success. Of all the departments a new employee might work for, yours becomes the one of choice.

> *You can accomplish anything you want as long as you let someone else take the credit.*
>
> Dr. Joe Mullins

Existing Organizational Structure

To successfully implement TQM in any corporation, you must first recognize its existing hierarchy. Later, in Chapter 5, I show how to transform that structure into the team that will enable TQM to succeed. A typical organizational hierarchy consists of three levels: (1) Executive, (2) Management, and (3) Workforce. A fourth entity, Key Executives, is also included as a subset of the Executive level. A description of each level within the organization follows below.

(1) Executive management includes those top-level managers who make up the top two layers of management within the corporation. Executive management begins with the Chief Executive Officer (CEO), and/or President, and one layer below. This second layer may include Directors or Vice Presidents (V.P.'s). In either case, this second layer of executive management maintains responsibility over functional areas within the organization. Key Executives make up a small portion of all executive management. This small cadre of individuals is routinely consulted first on important issues confronting the organization.

(2) Management includes people who supervise the workforce (directly or indirectly) and insure the completion of short-term

organization responsibilities. First-line supervisors are included here, as the lowest echelon of management.

(3) The workforce includes those individuals involved in the day-to-day activities of supporting the organization's function. If the organization is in the business of producing widgets, the workforce processes orders, turns wrenches, responds to customer complaints, packages and ships the product.

What Is a Process?

Webster's defines a process as a series of actions or operations that leads to a particular result. Similarly, in TQM, we define a process as a series of operations linked together to provide a result that has increased value. Refer to Exhibit 4. To the left, we put something into the process and to the right, we have an output, or a result with increased value. This increased value emerges from an exchange for resources. We most often include as resources people, equipment, material, money, and/or time. In a service company, we may have a purchase order entering a process that results in dispatching a team to repair a computer in the field. The process itself uses manpower to review the incoming purchase order, analyze the skills needed to address this particular problem, assign the work, and then dispatch the team to do its job. This one example demonstrates how an apparently simple, routine function plays an integral role in the performance of a computer-services department.

Prior to the computer repair ever being accomplished, a multitude of processes had to take place. A marketing department process spread the word--advertising to let potential consumers of our service, know we were in the business to meet their needs. In addition, the staff maintains qualified personnel to accomplish the actual repair. Therefore, before dispatching a team, the personnel department must identify the necessary qualifications for this person, advertise the position, schedule interviews, and accomplish all of the necessary paperwork activities so the selected candidate can become an associate of the company. Likewise, some processes are performed after the team has returned from successfully repairing the computer. These processes include invoicing the customer,

EXHIBIT 4.

The Process

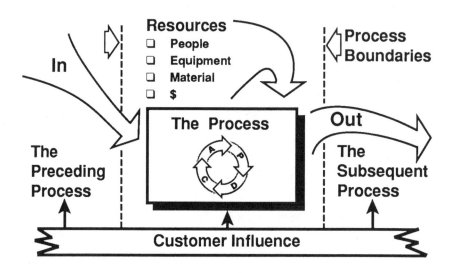

posting revenues in accounting, and of course, providing feedback to the team on its performance.

So, as you can see, one single process within an organization does not function alone. Rather, it interconnects many different processes within the company, allowing you to earn a reputation for excellent service. Factors that contribute and reinforce this view, from the customer's perspective, include courteous and efficient telephone personnel to receive the order, qualified and efficient repair personnel to meet with the customer to resolve the problem, and timely invoicing with appropriate follow-up and accounting. So, you can see, providing excellent customer service goes far beyond the individual in the field turning the wrench or installing a new belt. It is the smooth operation of many corporate relationships between the big ''C's'' and lots of little ''c's'' that allows the customer to conclude that you offer excellent service.

I wanted to walk through a service example here specifically because so many books on this subject focus on manufacturing examples. In manufacturing, we routinely think of the time it takes to perform an individual operation, such as installing a screw. This time, the operation-cycle time is the accumulation and inter-relationship of many operations that result in a cycle time for the entire process. These very same principles and concepts that allow us to streamline, optimize, and understand manufacturing processes apply directly to administrative and service processes as well.

To reiterate, a process is a series of operations linked together to provide a result that has increased value. We achieve this increased value in exchange for the expenditure of resources. What processes in your company add value and allow you to stay in business?

Before closing this section, I would like to mention one very important point. All processes have constraints. When designing a new process from scratch, we immediately form an impression of how to carry out this process. Then we encounter the process constraints. When transferring a process, such as moving purchasing from one building to another, you may be asked to perform the same or improved services with fewer resources. Fewer resources may mean less floor space. If your company recently cut back personnel, your constraint may be to perform the same job with fewer people, or a reduced budget. Regardless of the reason, you confront some constraints--challenges to do more with less. Understanding your processes and successfully applying the principles and tools of TQM allows you to respond to and successfully accommodate these new challenges.

Service versus Manufacturing Companies

One aspect of quality that has always intrigued me is the lack of attention to the subject in the service arena. When recognized gurus on the topic refer to the application of quality in service companies, they typically deal with it in the following way.

They consume one hundred pages or so using case studies, hard-hitting examples, and personal experiences showing how they have helped a manufacturing company improve. Without elaboration, they go on to describe, usually in a page or so, how the same principles and tools also apply to service companies. They routinely overlook two key points, which I would like to cover here.

33

First, when describing process improvement they often ignore the fact that many processes typically associated with these successes are not manufacturing-related at all. Yes, statistical process control was probably used to ensure the production of a quality part on the shop floor. In addition, other functions not traditionally associated with the manufacturing process directly contributed to the "quality" of that final part. These other administrative and support functions are typically overlooked. Some administrative functions that immediately come to mind include contracts, personnel, and maintenance. Administrative functions that always seem to lend themselves to improvement are procurement and the processing of Engineering Change Proposals (ECPs). There, the "boiler plate" has always prompted quality professionals to unlimited opportunities for process improvement. One of the most enlightening examples I have seen is in streamlining the processing of ECPs at the U.S. Air Force Aeronautical Systems Division (ASD). There, using some simple tools of TQM (ie. flow-charting) they reduced the time required to process ECPs by 40 percent, with the added benefit of saving 20 percent of the man-hours to accomplish the task.

"Boiler plate" usually means cut and splice from past contracts to yield a "standard" contract, with outdated requirements producing standardized results that are consistent with history. Bad! Under TQM, each contractual requirement is scrutinized for quality. Genuine requirements, those insuring a certain quality product or service, must be specified and the non-requirements deleted. The best example I can think of in this area applies to government contracts. It seems so easy to add additional requirements to each new contract to overcome a fluke, or one-of-a-kind occurrence that caused problems in the past. This management-by-exception has no place in a Total Quality organization and is presently being overcome by the government's own quality initiative (Hansen, Miller).

The personnel department is another support function that allows manufacturing operations to run smoothly. We have all heard the term "garbage in - garbage out" as it applies to computers. We must have good information entering the machine to produce quality results. This concept also applies to the corporate personnel function as well. In deploying Total Quality throughout, the personnel department becomes aware of its key role--insuring that personnel, our greatest resource, meet the quality we desire from team members. Total Quality companies recognize that hiring a new person is a *long-term investment*. The company maintains the responsibility of selling that individual on the long-term promise of his affiliation. As a company moves toward Total Quality, it begins to earn a reputation for excellence and can choose from the best employee prospects. When I think of companies that have already earned such a reputation, certain names come to mind. These names include Electronic Data Systems (EDS) in the computer services area, Sandia National Laboratories in Research and Development, and of course, the good name of IBM. Many people would like to work for these excellent companies or companies like them, but not everyone can. Is it your goal to work for an excellent company? Will you aid the process of transforming your company into an EDS or an IBM?

All companies, even manufacturing companies, have a mix of service and administrative functions that allows them to produce quality. The orchestration of all these functions, not just the shop floor functions themselves, enables them to produce quality. So what big differences between service and manufacturing companies should we account for when turning toward TQM? You will find these key points in Exhibit 5 (DiPrimio, 1987).

First, service companies have no product with exact specifications. Yes, they probably use some metric to tell them when they are on track, but this differs considerably from a manufactured product with critical dimensions and close tolerances. One example comes to mind from my own experience in technical consulting services, while with Booz Allen and Hamilton.

When selling a potential client on our services, we used "The Booz Allen Approach." It comprised our best effort to offer a structured methodology for problem solving. In the high technology arena, it is frequently difficult to predict what form the final product might take. So instead, we sold the client on our approach to the problem--identifying sources of information, critical decision points, etc. In doing so, we created an appreciation in the mind of our client that this was a new problem, one that had never been recognized before. We had our arms around an approach to deal with the problem and communicated our understanding of it. The Booz Allen Approach. This sharply contrasts a manufacturing problem, where the results appear in a drawing beforehand and the quality of the final product is measured with calipers.

EXHIBIT 5.

Service versus Manufacturing Organizations

❑ No Product with Exact Specifications
❑ Services are Perishable
❑ Strong Customer/Client Presence
❑ Delivery System

© Joseph R. Jablonski, 1990

Second, services are perishable. This became most apparent to me when President Reagan called for the technical expertise of this nation to be directed toward the Strategic Defense Initiative. Along with a shifting of government research dollars went the skills necessary to meet the challenge. The unavailability of the technical skills necessary to build this system soon became evident. Bomb designers for terrestrial systems aren't the same as the bomb designers for space systems. These special people had to be groomed to meet the technical services required for the conception and design of the new system. Technical skills are perishable, not readily transferable to what may appear to be a similar problem.

The third difference applies to the area of client/customer presence. In manufacturing, I can see a crate with a packing slip and invoice being received by the loading dock. Sometimes all producer/customer interaction takes place via letter and telephone with little or no direct, face-to-face contact. This is in sharp contrast to a service.

Let me continue the copier service example from early in the book. A copier repair person arrives at your facility, opens the machine, evaluates the problem, proceeds to open his/her tool case and goes to work. All along, office personnel watch, wondering how the repair person can solve the problem so quickly, with such a complicated device. For some reason, there is always a curiosity when equipment is opened that creates one-on-one interaction between the service person and the customer. This is also true if you offer a specialized technical service. Everyone in the meeting gathers around the consultant to gaze at the intricate drawings, understand every detail on the flow chart, and scrutinize every line of the computer print-out. In the services area, a real person stops by to deliver that service. The client/customer usually seizes the opportunity to ask questions, to better understand what is going on...to communicate.

The fourth contrasting factor between service and manufacturing is the delivery system involved. This extends from the discussion above on strong customer/client presence. Manufacturers commonly rely on the U.S. Postal Service as the delivery system for a component. Again, this differs from the delivery of a service, where a company representative usually does the delivering. This holds true for the delivery of a copier repair service, or the presentation of a methodology for solving a complex technological problem using the Booz Allen Approach.

In conclusion, differences do exist between service and manufacturing companies. However, the same features that make the delivery of services to the client/customer something special can be applied to manufacturing projects as well. Also, it should be evident that many of the things traditionally associated with service companies are embodied within manufacturing companies, in what we call ''administrative functions.'' Both differences and similarities exist. The understanding of these similarities and differences can help you become more competitive.

Overview: Implementation Approach

Exhibit 6 provides an overview to the five-phase process of implementing TQM in your corporation. Subsequent chapters describe each of these implementation phases in detail. Many of the questions that may surface in the interim will be addressed in reviewing the implementation schedule in Chapter 9. The schedule identifies interrelationships that must be maintained throughout implementation to insure a smooth transformation from your current status to your goal for the future.

EXHIBIT 6.

Overview

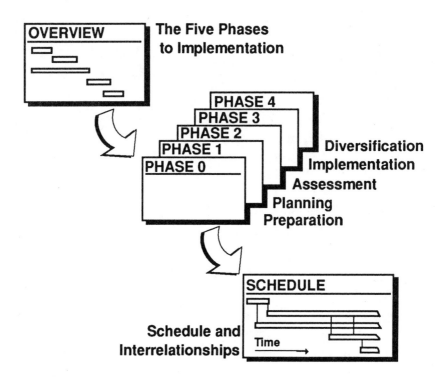

© Joseph R. Jablonski, 1990

Five Phases to Implementation

The following five phases are necessary for the successful implementation of TQM in your company:

Phase 0: Preparation

Phase 1: Planning

Phase 2: Assessment

Phase 3: Implementation

Phase 4: Diversification

Exhibit 7 displays all five phases and will help you understand their relative sequence of occurrence and interrelationships. As you can see, Phase 0 is unique in that it has a definite beginning and end. This differs from the other phases, which evolve over time and go on continuously.

EXHIBIT 7.

Five Phases to Implementation

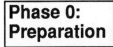

Phase 0: Preparation

Phase 1: Planning

Phase 2: Assessment

Phase 3: Implementation

Phase 4: Diversification

© Joseph R. Jablonski, 1990

Successful implementation of TQM begins with Phase 0, Preparation. It is termed Phase 0 because it actually precedes a building process involving the organization's Key Executives, with the aid of a professional facilitator. Here, the Key Executives develop the organization's vision statement, set corporate goals and draft policy in direct support of the corporate strategic plan. Phase 0 concludes with a commitment of resources necessary to plan the implementation of TQM.

The beginning of Phase 1, Planning, lays the foundation for the process of change within the organization. Here, individuals who will make up the Corporate Council use the statements developed during the Preparation Phase and begin the meticulous planning process. Once formed, the Corporate Council develops the implementation plan, commits resources and makes it a reality. The planning process relies on inputs from all subsequent phases to help guide its implementation and evolution.

Assessment, Phase 2, involves the exchange of information necessary to support the preparation, planning, implementation and diversification phases. It consists of surveys, evaluations, questionnaires and interviews throughout the organization at all levels as well as self-evaluations assessing individual and group perceptions of the organization's strengths and weaknesses.

Phase 3 is implementation. Here, the investments made during the previous phases pay off. A well-defined training initiative for managers and the workforce begins. With full support from the Corporate Council, Process Action Teams (PATs) are chartered to evaluate and improve processes and implement change.

The final phase, Phase 4, is diversification. Accomplishing Phase 0 (Preparation) through Phase 3 (Implementation) provides the organization with a substantial knowledge base. Policy has been defined, objections to change have been overcome, and success stories may already be reported by PATs. At this point, with newly acquired experience, other parts of the organization should be invited to participate. These others may include subordinate organizations, strategic business units, subsidiaries, off-site divisions, suppliers, vendors, or various departments within the organization. Diversification is recommended once credibility is earned by the parent implementing organization.

Top Management Commitment --
A Definition

When describing a company's commitment to change, all too often the person at the top fails to recognize the meaning of top management commitment. This major point is overlooked so often that I find it necessary to define precisely what it means.

Top management commitment is a commitment of corporate resources, including the executive's own time, to the improvement process. In fact, substantial amounts of executive time, particularly that of the CEO/President are necessary to successfully implement TQM. Committing a subordinate's time and corporate funds to this initiative is not enough. Both management and the workforce assess the importance of priorities in terms of where the CEO/President spends the majority of his or her time. It was said best by Peter F. Drucker, a recognized management expert, "Everything degenerates into work" (Drucker, 1974). Yes, that even applies to the person at the top.

Early in Phase 0, management spends time defining the organization's vision statement, detailing corporate goals, outlining policy and making that all-important decision to proceed into the planning phase. Although accomplished along with other senior executives, the active, hands-on participation of the senior executive is essential. These results spill over into the planning process, where the CEO/President creates and leads the Corporate Council, using his or her leadership to remove barriers which would otherwise make the responsibilities across an organization's functional boundaries irreconcilable. The person at the top must routinely voice support and enthusiasm for TQM, play a decisive role in recognizing contributors to the implementation process, participate in manager training, and create a proactive, positive image of TQM in the minds of everyone in the organization. Just as the company demonstrates TQM prior to expecting others to do it in the Diversification Phase, the CEO/President should also demonstrate TQM prior to expecting it of his or her people. You lead by example.

41

Where Others Have Failed or Fumbled

So many books describe success and how to improve that we often forget there are some failures among all the successes. Not all experiences are positive, but we can learn from them if they lead to intangible benefits for those involved. This section discusses where others have encountered difficulty in implementing TQM, so we might learn.

It is timely to review this important topic now, since we can relate directly to the five-phase implementation methodology above and avoid some common pitfalls. For review, there are five phases in the TQM process: (1) Preparation, (2) Planning, (3) Assessment, (4) Implementation, and (5) Diversification. Each phase has the possibility for problems if not handled correctly. Let us review the most common errors I have witnessed from observing the implementation of change.

Phase 0 - Preparation. The most common error Key Executives make here is the decision to proceed. Some believe you can actually make the wrong decision to implement corporate-wide change. From my experience, failure only arises from making a half-decision. That is, a half-hearted effort to implement TQM when you, yourself, are not thoroughly convinced of its benefits. Presidents or CEOs who delegate this important initiative to a subordinate have not understood the importance of top management commitment. They treat it like any other program where they are briefed on progress, cost, and schedule, without taking an active part in making it a reality. This is where many fail. If TQM, as a major, corporate initiative, is neither approved nor disapproved, but rather put in place with half-hearted, half steps, it cannot succeed. We observe striking examples of this point in government's efforts to move toward Total Quality. Regulations and directives motivate few, if any, people. Therefore, the challenge in government is to convince individual organizations of the need for change. In the private sector this is not too difficult. Either people produce, or the company folds. In government the difficulty is convincing each and every individual of the need for change and showing him how he will benefit by helping the change take place. That is a tough thing to do.

Phase 1, Planning, is another place where corporate executives can cause themselves heartache. In this phase the goal is to begin the downward deployment of TQM and involve all corporate executives. Failures sometimes occur from not providing enough time or incentive to convince all executives of the need for this change. All executives must accept this process and begin to appreciate the magnitude of the change that is about to take place. If everyone involved in the planning phase is not convinced of a meaningful gain by implementing TQM, fall back, regroup, and go through the drill again until everyone agrees. Lee Iacocca says, "Commitment to quality is like a commitment to religion. It pervades everything (by necessity)" (Iacocca, 1984).

Phase 2, Assessment. This phase requires a strong sense of self-security, asking your people for feedback on the strengths and weaknesses of the organization and comments on how they interpret your leadership at the management and workforce levels. The greatest challenge to the corporate executive here is committing the time and money to having a proper organizational assessment conducted. Though many aspects of the Assessment phase can be accomplished by in-house personnel, the organizational assessment cannot. This can become another pitfall for many companies; top management surveys personnel, asking difficult questions that are best handled by an independent person with no vested interest in the outcome. To avoid this potential pitfall, I suggest you seek and retain the best talent available to accomplish the organizational assessment. It is important.

Phase 3, Implementation. A common problem occurs when mass training is begun for all management and workforce personnel before resolving some very basic issues. These issues, which may insure success or failure, result directly from what has happened in the three previous phases. Before group training begins in Phase 3, two things must have been accomplished:

(1) all executives must be in "sync" as to the need and importance of implementing TQM. Everyone, including the President/CEO, must be convinced that something valuable will be gained from making TQM happen, and;

(2) the results from the organizational assessment must be used in the planning process (Phase 1) to ascertain the training needs of the organization. While much of the initial TQM training is fairly standard, terminology, pinpointing specific cases, and other factors must be considered in tailoring this information to consumption for management and workforce personnel. Then, and only then, will people depart a TQM training session with a positive feeling that what has just been covered applies to them.

These pitfalls do not necessarily dictate failure, but they can short-circuit your best intentions and postpone the realization of that first success story by six months, a year, or more. If these remarks are taken as intended, you will be safe in the knowledge you did not reinvent some of the failures experienced by others.

What if the CEO Isn't Committed?

This one topic has been the source of great frustration for me, personally. At one time, if confronted by an uncommitted CEO/ president, I would have thrown up my hands and said, ''Let's just forget it and part as friends right now.'' Unfortunately, life isn't that simple, and there are many good reasons to pursue TQM, even if certain individuals are not sold on the idea. Although an uncommitted CEO/president dictates failure for TQM as a corporate-wide initiative, this does not mean the pursuit of Total Quality is impossible for everyone in the organization. However certain limits must be understood.

We have all seen examples of Total Quality at some level within our company. These examples of excellence may include a Directorate, Department, or Section. The most obvious indicators that such a special entity exists within our own company are as follows.

Everyone works hard; they're challenged; they appreciate the opportunity to excel; and everyone is trying to become part of that group. They're winners. The group leader possesses unique management skills which allow him or her to practice the principles and philosophy of Total Quality, even though he or she may have had no focused training in this area. The leader may send the people to training sessions, special instruction to enhance their ability to

44

work as a team and improve internal processes. We have here an excellent example of Total Quality in action. That's the good news.

The not-so-good news is that's where it ends. The supervisor can directly influence that group's ability to perform and improve processes within their own domain. Difficulties come into play when supervisors try to improve processes, or portions of processes, outside their immediate area of responsibility and are affected by the results. An example in purchasing comes to mind. It is one thing to recognize the need for a new piece of equipment that would significantly enhance the throughput of your department and be ready to use at a moment's notice. Unfortunately, Purchasing, who would deliver the packaged equipment, still operates under the "business as usual" philosophy, taking six months to respond to such an order. You're stuck. You must then have a higher level of support and recognize your individual limitations in making Total Quality happen.

Chapter 4. Phase 0: Preparation

Decision to Consider TQM

The most important phase in the implementation process is Phase 0, where corporate Key Executives decide if they will consider whether they could benefit from the sweeping improvements possible from TQM. They obtain initial training, develop the organization's vision statement and corporate goals, draft corporate policy, commit initial resources, and prepare a speech to convey this important message. The sequence of these events includes the seven-step process described in Exhibit 8. The length of these steps does not imply their relative duration; they merely denote the logical sequence of events one would follow to successfully accomplish Phase 0. In contrast to the other four phases, Phase 0 has a definite beginning and ending point.

The first step is a decision to consider implementing TQM. This decision can range from ''let's do it'' to ''let's consider implementing TQM.'' Perhaps a Key Executive has been inspired by the successes of a competitor, or has been directed to do so by a major customer. Whatever the reason, training, must follow.

Key Executive Training

Training, Step 2, is where a large fraction, preferably the entire Key Executive staff, undergoes initial TQM training. It can occur either off-site, or on the organization's premises. I prefer off-site training with all Key Executives in attendance. It is important that all Key Executives view concurrently, so they can better understand the benefits of TQM to their organization with the advantage of training interaction among them.

EXHIBIT 8.

Phase 0: Preparation

△ **Decision to Consider TQM**

△ **Key Executive Training**

△ **Develop Vision Statement**

Develop Corporate Goals △

Outline Corporate Policy △

Decision to Proceed △
Commit Initial Resources

Speech Prepared △

© Joseph R. Jablonski, 1990

During this training, several important things are accomplished. First, Key Executives begin aligning their thinking with the philosophy of TQM. For some, these concepts may be new and their application not readily apparent. For this reason, a professional facilitator should encourage a high level of interaction. It is important to overcome the fear of change and address individual resistance to this new way of doing business. These issues will surface later with your subordinates, and you must be prepared to deal with them.

It is also important to define and refine the terminology the company will use. For instance, I have heard many terms used to describe the resource approval and team empowerment entity for TQM. Some refer to it as the Quality Committee, the Quality Council, whatever. I prefer the term Corporate Council and am reluctant to refer to most anything as a committee. What you call it may not be as important as selecting and agreeing upon terminology you can relate to. Many fumble in this one area. They use several sources of training for TQM, fail to coordinate terminology, and hence confuse a lot of people with a lot of different terms. This becomes an important point as you begin the downward deployment of TQM throughout your organization. Everyone must be reading off the same sheet of music.

Corporate Strategic Planning

I have read enough on this subject to become thoroughly confused. So let me explain my perception of a corporate strategic plan and draw the connection between it and TQM.

Every company must have a purpose, a reason to be in business. I call it the Corporate Mission. Routinely, when thinking about the future of your company, you may be drawing a picture of a company that doesn't exactly coincide with its present product, service, or position within the industry. That's OK! That's your Corporate Vision--a statement of where you want to be in the future. It is that vital link between your mission and vision that I call the strategic plan. This is the road map that guides you to that new company, which presently exists only in your mind.

Exhibit 9 shows the division of responsibilities and elements necessary to put a corporate strategic plan in place. It all begins with the CEO/President defining the Corporate Vision. This vision translates into a set of Corporate Objectives. Some objectives such as "Penetrate New Market," are long-term and may take five to ten years to be realized. Others, such as "Reduce Customer Complaints," may be short-term, with visible signs of results being sought almost immediately. Corporate Goals translate into the tasks and eventually measurable parameters that are gathered by management and workforce personnel. The downward deployment of this information conveys what is important to employees at all levels within the organization. Follow-up actions and their results can then be communicated back up through the corporate hierarchy. A comparison is made between the expectations and the actual results obtained; the necessary adjustments are made so as to keep the company on course. This important element of feedback, communication between different levels within the company, maintains a constant alignment between the highest and lowest levels in the organization. As you will see, the CEO/President uses the Corporate Vision to communicate to all employees what is valued, what is important, and where the company is going.

> *You've removed most of the road-blocks to success when you've learnt the difference between motion and direction.*

Bill Copeland

EXHIBIT 9

Division of Responsibilities

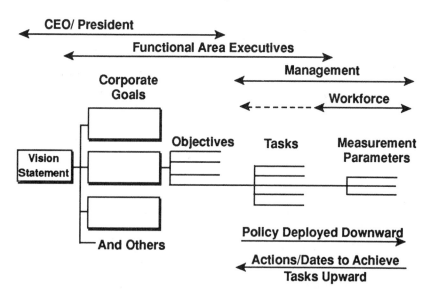

© Joseph R. Jablonski, 1990

Develop Vision Statement

Development of the organization vision statement is the first positive step toward TQM. Ideally, this takes place during a brainstorming session, typically off-site, with the aid of a trained professional facilitator. Here, via consensus, Key Executives arrive at a brief, concise statement as to why they are in business. It is normally expressed in terms of a commitment to quality, responsiveness to customer requirements, and becoming more competitive. Exhibit 10 provides some examples.

Development of the corporate vision statement always seems to give executives great difficulty. I like to use the following technique to meet the challenge. (1) Have each Key Executive brainstorm one ingredient, one term that is important for the vision statement and without which a major, important point would be lost. (2) Draw the group to a prioritized list of things that should be embodied in the vision statement. (3) Use that list as an outline of the vision statement and have groups develop several versions of how it should read. (4) Allow everyone to eventually arrive at a final product through iteration and consensus. I have shown some important terms in the examples listed in Exhibit 10. These include:

> "provide products that conform to our customers' requirements,"

> "do the job right the first time," and

> "deliver error-free competitive products on time."

My favorite is "we work together." I like it because it emphasizes the team aspect of our definition of TQM. "We work together!"

The vision statement must be easy to understand so everyone in the organization can relate to its meaning and his/her role in its success. I cannot overemphasize the importance of brevity. The "Lord's Prayer" contains 56 words, "Lincoln's Gettysburg Address" 268, yet the "Federal Government Regulation on the Sale of Cabbage" 26,911. Enough said.

EXHIBIT 10.

Examples of Organization Vision Statements

"We are the Aeronautical Systems Division, the center of excellence for research, development and acquisition of systems. We work together to create quality systems for combat capability to ensure we remain the best Air Force in the world and preserve the American way of life forever."

United States Aeronautical Systems
Division, Wright Patterson AFB, Ohio

"The policy of the Midwestern Steel Division of Armco is to provide products that conform to our customers' requirements and deliver them on time and at a competitive price. Our name must represent quality to our vendors, ourselves, and to our customers."

Armco, Inc.
Midwest Steel Division

"In order to improve quality we shall provide clearly stated requirements, expecting each person to do the job right the first time, in accordance with those requirements or cause the requirements to be officially changed."

Bechtel
Ann Arbor Power Division

"We shall strive for excellence in all endeavors. We shall set our goals to achieve total customer satisfaction and to deliver error-free competitive products on time, with service second to none."

Burroughs

"We will deliver defect-free competitive products and services on time to our customers."

IBM
Research Triangle Park, Raleigh

"Milliken and Company is dedicated to providing products and services designed to be at a level of quality which will best help its customers grow and prosper. Its operational area (Research and Development, Marketing, Manufacturing, Administration, Services) will be expected to perform its functions exactly as written in carefully prepared specifications."

Milliken

Develop Corporate Goals

The corporate goals must flow from the organization vision statement described above. There may be many goals but, again, they must be concise. Exhibit 11 provides an example of an organization's corporate goals. From this sample, you see that the focus of this organization's corporate goals touches every aspect of the organization--from retaining technical excellence in its people, to maintaining a safe work environment.

I included Goal 0, "Implement TQM," to stimulate your thinking. It seems almost automatic for corporate executives to place this on their list of corporate goals. I mention this because I believe goals should be fluid, dynamic, changing with time. The corporate executive who places "Implement TQM" on this list may later discover that it needs to remain there forever. If removed, it can be construed that TQM is done, accomplished, finished. And as we all know, real TQM is a continuous process that goes on forever. So be aware of the perceptions you create in the minds of your people.

Outline Corporate Policy

Step 5 involves outlining corporate policy concerning TQM. A successful definition of policy accurately conveys to the workforce the resolve of corporate leaders to see TQM succeed. Key Executives will form the "skeleton" of policy, determining what is important and what is not. The "body" takes shape as it develops in Phase 1 by the Corporate Council. Here, the traditional system of rewards and recognition will change dramatically. Typically, subordinates are rewarded for accomplishments. The definition of accomplishment may expand to include those individuals who attempted to apply a TQM principle or use a TQM tool and maybe fell short of the expectations. This presents an opportunity to emphasize that something less than "success" may be a step in the right direction, and that individuals should be recognized for their best efforts in a positive way.

Some other policy issues that must be addressed include job security and management support. Job security is crucial today, as more and more companies downsize. This poses a genuine threat

EXHIBIT 11.

Corporate Goals

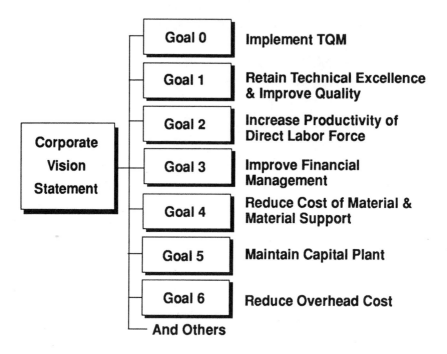

Goal 0	**Implement TQM**
Goal 1	**Retain Technical Excellence & Improve Quality**
Goal 2	**Increase Productivity of Direct Labor Force**
Goal 3	**Improve Financial Management**
Goal 4	**Reduce Cost of Material & Material Support**
Goal 5	**Maintain Capital Plant**
Goal 6	**Reduce Overhead Cost**

Corporate Vision Statement

And Others

to everyone in the organization. For this reason, workers need assurance that they will not lose their jobs as a result of a productivity gain realized through TQM. Rather, people resources will be brought to bear on other compelling needs within the company. This point must remain separate and distinct from the company's need to trim down on payroll due to economic downturns. This is a tough issue.

Management support can be best conveyed by giving subordinates an opportunity to be heard at the top. A review entity must be formed to prioritize suggestions for consideration by the Corporate Council. The perceived fairness of this group will play a key role in whether or not people four levels into the organization really feel they have a pipeline to the top. This represents the executive link between themselves, management, and the workforce.

Decision to Proceed

The sixth step in Phase 0 is a decision and a commitment of resources. Here, after completing the previous five steps, the Key Executives elect to pursue implementation of TQM. This is done by committing resources to accomplish part of Phase 1, Planning. At this point, other executives in the company become exposed to and involved with TQM. Involvement of the Key Executives is not over; they will soon make other decisions in Phase 1, concerning the expenditure of resources for full implementation.

The importance of the decision to commit resources cannot be understated. This is a potential pitfall, where many fail. Without full commitment, the CEO/President proceeds on to Phase 1 without making it absolutely clear that an important, far-reaching decision has been made. Some of the more popular techniques employed by the CEO/President to avoid making this important decision are (1) "I need more data" and (2) "I'll put someone else in charge." Both are potentially fatal.

"More data" is my favorite. This is where the CEO/President, unsure of his or her position, avoids the inevitable by merely asking for more and more data. This stall tactic results in dismal failure and a lack of credibility on future endeavors. The go-ahead to proceed onto Phase 1 must be approached with enthusiasm--a religious fervor that TQM can truly benefit the organization. No degree of cost-benefit analysis, trade-off studies or justification can sway disbelievers. Remember, if you had all the information you desired, you probably wouldn't need a CEO/President. Decide. Make a decision, even if you choose to scrap the whole idea. That decision is better than no decision at all.

Putting someone else in charge is not an answer either. Corporate policy and direction are undelegatable. . .if that's a word. When conducting training on TQM, individuals in the audience always discuss who is in attendance at this and earlier training sessions. They especially notice the presence or absence of the most senior people in the organization. That is not unreasonable. Roland Peterson, President of Litton Industries, recently completed their 26-hour team training during a regularly scheduled class in June

1989. His remarks after completing the class are inspiring.

> "I now understand from the inside how Perfect Teams work."

He goes on to say,

> "This will make it much easier for me to communicate the advantages of employee involvement to other divisions."

You, as a leader, must participate in the training process if you intend to convince subordinates of your resolve and communicate the importance of this valued initiative.

Are You Making Progress?

In Chapter 1, I described the tell-tale signs of a problem company and used the term Un-quality. Two questions often brought up by executives are, "How do I know when I am making improvements in my company?" and "What do I look for to convince myself that we are on track toward Total Quality?" Just as you can recognize traits that suggest room for improvement, you can also observe things that indicate you are on the path to Total Quality. I will describe them here.

Exhibit 12 offers a summary of factors that contribute to Total Quality. As you can see, there are eight Quality Factors: Top Management Commitment, Obsession with Excellence, Organization Is Customer-Satisfaction Driven, etc. For each of these Quality Factors, you can categorize your own corporate quality position with a numerical value from 1 to 5, with 5 representing Total Quality. Let us review some of these quality factors so that you can recognize them easily. Once you use this information to identify how you, as a company, stack up today, you have taken an important step toward Total Quality. We refer to this as Benchmarking-- understanding where you are. Once benchmarked, you can begin using the tools of TQM to identify areas for improvement, prioritize opportunity, and measure your progress through the other categories.

Most companies begin at or near category 1. They consider inspection a primary tool to insure against defective products and services leaving the facility. With the focus on inspection, no one considers how the defects could be prevented from occurring in the first place. Some companies believe increased quality translates directly into increased costs, without recognizing the potential savings that could be realized from defect prevention. They spend time correcting errors, and their quality initiative is isolated to a handful of professionals within the manufacturing department. Statistical Process Control is considered an isolated tool, probably for the control of a manufacturing process. The thought of defect prevention is foreign to these companies.

As top management commitment takes hold and TQM is accepted as a new way of doing business, a balance is struck between long-term goals and short-term objectives. Adequate money and time are allocated to training and continuous process improvement. As you move closer toward a Total Quality company, certain things surface as a routine way of doing business. Eventually, the continuous improvement becomes a natural behavior. Teams are formed with representation from different functional groups, and they work together.

As customer service becomes a driving goal, more customers seek to establish long-term relationships. They want you to become a strategic supplier. Now you have suppliers with qualified and quantified improvements from their benchmarked initial beginnings within their own Total Quality process.

Statistics and Statistical Process Control have become a common language, rather than something retained on the shop floor. Employees and managers alike understand process flow and process variation. They communicate with a consistent language, making things better for everyone. The challenge of change toward TQM is great, but so are the rewards.

Corporate Speech

It appears to have begun with Lee Iacocca, then Victor Kiam. Today it seems almost commonplace for the corporate leaders,

EXHIBIT 12.

Benchmarking Matrix

TQM Category	A Top Management Commitment	B Obsession with Excellence	C Organization is Customer - Satisfaction Driven	D Supplier Involvement
1		Traditional Approach to Quality Control: ☐ Inspection is Primary Tool (Control of Defects, Not Prevention) ☐ Better Quality = Higher Cost	☐ Quality Control Found Only in Manufacturing Departments ☐ Significant Scrap and Rework Activity	Suppliers Know Your TQM Direction; Supplier Number Reduction Started
2	Balance of Long-Term Goals with Short-Term Objectives	Corporate Council Set Up	Customer Rating of Company Is Known	Suppliers Know Your TQM Direction; Supplier Number Reduction Started
3	Adequate Money and Time Allocated to Continuous Improvement and Training	TQM Support System Set Up and in Use	Customer Feedback Used in Decision Making	Direct Involvement in Supplier Awareness Training; Supplier Criteria in Place
4	Focus is on Improving the System	Use of Cross-Functional Improvement Teams	Striving to Improve Value to Customers is a Routine Behavior	Suppliers Actively Implementing TQM Philosophy
5	Continuous Improvement is a Natural Behavior Even during Routine Tasks	Constant, Relative Improvement in Quality, Cost, and Productivity	Customer Satisfaction is the Primary Goal. More Customers Desire Long-Term Relationship	Suppliers Fully Qualified in All Benchmark Areas

Source: Defense Dept.

58

EXHIBIT 12. (CONT.)

Benchmarking Matrix

TQM Category	E Continuous Learning	F Employee Involvement	G Use of Incentives	H Use of Tools
1		Traditional Approach to Quality Control: □ *SPC Used as an Example, Other Tools Identified Separately □ November 14, 1989		
2	Training Plan Developed	Manager Presents Ideas and Invites Questions, Makes Decision	Effective Employee Suggestion Program Used	SPC* Used in Manufacturing
3	Ongoing Training Programs	Manager Presents Problem, Gets Suggestions, Makes Decisions	Quality Related Employee Selections and Promotion Criteria	SPC* Used for Variation Reduction
4	Top Management Understands and Applies TQM Philosophy	Manager Defines Limits; Asks Group to Make Decisions	More Team than Individual Incentives and Rewards	More Team than Individual Incentives and Rewards
5	Training in TQM Tools Common among All Employees	People Involvement; Self-Directing Work Groups	Gainsharing (Cross-Functional Work Groups)	Statistics is a Common Language Among All Employees

Source: Defense Dept.

Presidents and CEOs to be highly visible in promoting their cause. Lee Iacocca sold America on the "New Chrysler Corporation." Victor Kiam liked the company so much he bought it. Executives recognize more and more that if they want their message heard, they better be the ones doing the talking.

> *To be persuasive, we must be believable.*
> *To be believable, we must be credible.*
> *To be credible, we must be truthful.*
>
> Edward R. Murrow

To effectively communicate this message you must (1) know what the message is, (2) believe it yourself, and (3) deliver it yourself. All three things can be difficult for the corporate executive.

At the top of the list, you must know what the message is. If you have successfully arrived at this point in the TQM implementation process with a corporate vision statement you believe in, you are well on your way. You can transform it into a brief presentation you initially offer as a "canned speech." Later, as you refine your presentation, the script goes away and you will speak from the heart. I have included a speech I like as an example in Exhibit 13. Of course I like it--I wrote it.

Points number two and three--belief and delivery--are frequently overlooked. Before becoming an independent trainer and consultant I worked for the government for six years. There, I learned the value of having the person at the top convey support for an initiative by promoting it himself. Mistakes I have frequently seen include delegating the communication responsibility to a subordinate, or using a routine communication mechanism where the importance of the message can easily be lost. Often routine communication from the top is accomplished via memos. If the CEO/President uses that same mechanism to convey the importance of TQM, something bad will happen. Let me give you an example. Let's say the CEO/President conveys his or her new thrust, a major initiative of great importance, conveyed by memo through the "chain of command."

Unbeknownst to the CEO/President, these memos are received at such a frequency that their level of importance has diminished. They become routine. The employee places the memo in a convenient location, along with all of the other "important" messages received over the past few months. Therefore, if TQM is really important to you, you must communicate the message by some means which sets it apart from all other messages. Nothing works quite as well as your personal presence.

> *Three things matter in a speech; who says it, how he says it, and what he says, and of the three, the last matters least.*

> John Morley

EXHIBIT 13.

Example Corporate Speech

I feel that each one of us at Technical Management Consortium (TMC) must promise Quality to our clients. This is a commitment of on-going value by TMC. Our pledge is to provide error-free, interested and knowledgeable service to each client throughout the service life cycle. This pledge applies to each and every employee. This pledge of QUALITY sets us apart from others whose goals are short-term versus our on-going, long-term vision. In these days of mediocre service and lack of attention to detail, it is paramount for all of us to make this pledge and commitment of QUALITY to remind us of what our clients expect of us when they come to TMC.

Joseph R.Jablonski
President
March 1989

Chapter 5. Phase 1: Planning

Overview

During this phase the detailed implementation plan is developed, the supporting structure put in place, and resources committed to accomplish implementation. Along with committing resources, another important decision occurs--determining the strategy for implementing TQM. Exhibit 14 summarizes the steps necessary to accomplish Phase 1, Planning. This phase requires the largest number of steps. The planning phase continues to develop the foundation upon which success stories will be derived later.

Steps 1 and 2 of the Planning Phase involve propagating the spirit of TQM beyond the small cadre of Key Executives in Phase 0, to include all executive managers. Individuals now brought into the improvement process include all Corporate Council members as well as the TQM Coordinator. For the most part, members of the Council will be selected from the existing organizational chart. Not so for the TQM Coordinator. He or she will be hand-picked to serve as the ''glue'' that bonds together all aspects of this important initiative. The selection of this person should not be done in haste, as he or she will maintain a prominent position toward the top of the organizational chart commensurate with his or her responsibility.

I listened to the president of Maryland Bank speak on their quality initiatives during the October 1989 National Quality Forum.

Impressed with his presentation, I decided to call his company and speak to the person in charge of quality. I was immediately transferred to their quality advocate, who proceeded to tell me about the advantages of their services, their turn-around time to replace stolen or missing credit cards, and the quality parameter they use to measure performance in the customer service department--the number of telephone rings before answering. She then tried to sell me on their MasterCard. I was impressed by the way they strive to satisfy the needs of their customers. As it turned out, she was a vice president. Not surprisingly, companies successful in Total Quality always manage to assign the appropriate rank structure with the position.

In Step 3, Training, Council members not trained in Phase 0 will be trained along with the TQM Coordinator. As in Phase 0, this training includes an introduction to the principles and concepts of

EXHIBIT 14.

Phase 1: Planning

△ **Select Corporate Council Members**
△ **Select TQM Coordinator**
　　　　△ **Train Corporate Council & TQM Coordinator**
　　　△ **1st Corporate Council Meeting**
　　　　　△ **Draft Implementation Plan**
Approve Plan & Commit Resources △
Identify Critical Processes & Objectives △
　　　　Select Implementation Strategy △
　　　　Support Services On Board △

© Joseph R. Jablonski, 1990

TQM, with some exposure to the tools peculiar to TQM. To insure a broad-based understanding of the management aspects the TQM Coordinator should receive supplemental training on management and tools of TQM as well as facilitation. This knowledge will prove useful because the TQM Coordinator, in his or her full-time capacity, will facilitate meetings regularly, advise all levels within the organization, and match consulting support with the specific needs of Process Action Teams. The traits to consider when selecting the TQM Coordinator are included in Exhibit 15. As you can see, this requires a very special person.

EXHIBIT 15.

Facilitator Selection Criteria

1. A mix of personnel from different levels within the orginization.

2. People who have credibility.

3. People with a track record of successufully introducing innovation and achieving organizational commitment.

4. People who are known to be team players and have the leadership capacity to bring together the thinking of the group.

5. People with good interpersonal and communication skills.

6. Volunteers! They must really want to do this.

7. People who have a strong personal belief in the participative ethic.

8. People who can constructively confront the status quo and still work effectively with those in positions of authority.

9. People who are self-secure and able to maintain clear thinking in conflict situations.

10. People who will be around for a while.

© Joseph R. Jablonski, 1990

Once the Corporate Council members and the TQM Coordinator have been selected and trained, they can proceed to their first TQM Council Meeting. Specific items that should be discussed during the first Corporate Council meeting include the Council's charter, division of responsibilities necessary to support the implementation plan, and upcoming schedule of events, to name only a few. A sample agenda for this first meeting is included in Exhibit 16. This meeting will serve as the first opportunity to involve the workforce and introduce them to the improvement process. One management technique is to have a representative or two from the workforce participate in Council proceedings, either as regular members or as advisors on specific agenda items.

Next, the draft TQM Implementation Plan is prepared. This involves the direct participation of all Council members, as well as specific inputs from the workforce. The overall coordination and integration task will be the responsibility of the TQM Coordinator. The section on training becomes quite important. Here, active involvement of the organization training representative is essential. The review, selection, and implementation of the training program will be the responsibility of the Training Department, with inputs from the Council, workforce, and TQM Coordinator.

Approval of the implementation plan will transpire smoothly if everyone participates in its development, and there are no last-minute surprises. The difficulty comes in committing resources. The issue of money always seems to be a problem, but here it is an especially sensitive issue, due to the magnitude of the dollars involved. It may require a reallocation of budgets within the organization, or a request for support from a senior organization. Regardless of how this is accomplished, it should be recognized that this is a long-term investment from which the organization can expect a substantial return.

After the plan's approval, the next step is identifying the critical processes within the organization and their link to corporate goals. If you cannot draw a direct link between your processes and corporate goals, this is the time to make the necessary adjustments. The tools of TQM can aid you here. Brainstorming, facilitation,

EXHIBIT 16.

Sample Agenda for First Corporate Council Meeting

- ❑ Call Meeting to Order

- ❑ Introduce Council Members

- ❑ Introduce TQM Coordinator

- ❑ Review Roles & Responsibilities of Council Members & TQM Coordinator

- ❑ Review Draft Charter

- ❑ Review Upcoming Schedule of Events

  Implementation Plan Draft Due

  Implementation Plan Approval

  Selection of Implementation Strategy

  Identification of Critical Processes & Objectives

  Support Services On Board

  Speech Preparation

- ❑ Define Division of Responsibilities to Prepare Implementation Plan

- ❑ Schedule Next Meeting

- ❑ Adjourn Meeting

© Joseph R. Jablonski, 1990

group dynamics--many of the qualitative and quantitative tools of TQM will play an important role in Phase 1.

Next, the Council selects an implementation strategy. This criteria will be used to select problems for the PATs. You may consider four basic approaches:

1. The Top-Down Approach
2. Good Ideas from Employees
3. Customer Suggestions
4. Chronic Problems

The Top-Down approach provides a logical audit trail from the organization's vision statement, through goals, to objectives and assignment of PATs. PATs are assigned based upon a demonstrated relationship between problem resolution and corporate objectives. This is a good approach from an accounting perspective, but it can be difficult to get PAT support and personal commitment from the workforce. Because the ideas generally belong to someone else, this approach is more consistent with a management style that was in place before TQM.

Option 2 is one of my favorites, supporting good ideas from the employees. Getting employees to "buy into" the improvement process is not an easy task. Workforce resistance can be overcome if the Council supports an employee's idea and provides the necessary resources to succeed. Everyone wins under this option.

Option 3, a customer suggestion, should not be ignored. Mr. Joe Girard, "The Greatest Salesman in the World," according to *Guinness Book of World Records*, suggests that one dissatisfied customer has the ability to turn away up to 250 potential customers. Furthermore, most customers don't complain to you. They complain to their friends, and they just don't come back (Girard, 1979). For these reasons and more, you should make every effort to keep good customers by showing them immediate results when resolving their complaint. A complaining customer, despite conventional wisdom, is an asset and may surface opportunities for process improvement that have been overlooked by your own people.

Finally, Option 4 is the Chronic Problem. This is a problem that has plagued your organization for as long as anyone can remember; it costs both money and time, creating frustration regularly. I suggest postponing these problems until professional help arrives, or until after you have experienced some successes in process improvement. It is unlikely that any individual within the organization will possess the necessary objectivity and skill to tackle such problems early in the implementation of TQM; this is where hired consultants can be put to good use. Moreover, attacking this type of problem early on can easily result in failure, which impedes progress toward TQM in the future.

A summary of the four problem selection criteria, as well as some pros and cons of each, is included in Exhibit 17. Personal experience causes me to favor Options 2 and 3 above. I've found it preferable to support the ideas of the workforce and customers first. A simple explanation clarifies that statement. If you, as an organization leader or Council member, support your employees and customers early on, you will probably have sufficient time to tackle the bigger problems in the future. The reverse is not always true.

I will close with two pointers for easing the burden of selecting problems to be addressed by PATs: (1) Offer a clear path to success for the first few problems you address. This means that after your people have been trained, a light may go off in their heads; you'll hear a snap of the fingers; and someone will say, "Wasn't that obvious?" That is an easy candidate for TQM. (2) Early on, all TQM PATs should be able to see the light at the end of the tunnel. There will be time to repair the big problems in the future. In the beginning, look for quick turn-around time to gain feedback from your successes, as well as the things that have not gone exactly as expected. To emphasize, initially select TQM projects which insure a clear path towards success and quick turn-around time.

Forming the Team

To successfully implement TQM in any organization, the existing organization hierarchy must be transformed into the team that will make TQM a reality. This renewed structure will become one of

EXHIBIT 17.

Problem Selection Criteria Options Available to the Corporate Council

Options	Pros	Cons
Top Down	Relates PAT assignments directly to Organization Vision Statement.	Risks overlooking compelling or more costly problems.
Good Idea from Employee	Supports and encourages more ideas from employees.	Employee offering the suggestion may feel overlooked if his idea is not selected.
Customer Suggestion	"The customer is always right."	Mechanism must be in place to provide feedback to organization.
Chronic Problem	Everyone recognizes this is a long term problem which must be resolved.	May be too difficult to tackle in the early phases.

© Joseph R. Jablonski, 1990

three elements included in Exhibit 18--the Corporate Council, Process Action Teams (PATs), and Support Services.

In the end, all business operations can be reduced to three words: people, product, and profits. People come first.   Unless you've got a good team, you can't do much with the other two (Iacocca, 1984).

Lee Iacocca

Corporate Council

The Corporate Council consists of a leader and the organization's functional managers. The leader is the CEO or President. Functional managers, the next layer below the CEO/President, may be Vice-Presidents, Directors, etc. Remember, the Council includes

EXHIBIT 18.

Team Elements Necessary to Implement TQM

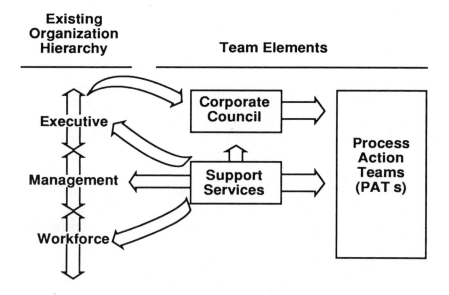

© Joseph R. Jablonski, 1990

those individuals who actively participated in Phase 0. The Council now has the responsibility to develop and implement policy, to develop and implement the TQM plan, and to create, empower and support PATs. The Council also reviews, analyzes, and improves processes within the organization with the aid of PATs and the advice of the TQM Coordinator. **The greatest responsibility of the Council is to remove barriers between functional entities within the organization and facilitate communication to show support and overcome the resistance PATs will inevitably encounter.** Council members are trained prior to creating the first PAT.

Process Action Teams

Process Action Teams are chartered by the Council as a result of their having selected a process for improvement. Commonly, one member of the PAT will have suggested the idea being addressed. PATs include a mixture of workforce, management, and executives; the Council selects the exact composition. To facilitate communications for processes involving more than one functional area, the Council may select a PAT member from each affected functional area. One PAT member will be selected to lead the group. That person may not necessarily represent the highest ranking individual from the organization. Rather, he or she is selected by peers among the PAT participants.

Support Services

This element includes the top TQM individual within the organization, the TQM Coordinator, as well as a mixture of consulting and training services. Organizationally, the TQM Coordinator resides at a level directly below the CEO and/or President in a staff role at parity with the deputy or a senior V.P. It is the full-time responsibility of the TQM Coordinator, with the aid of others in Support Services, to serve as arms, legs, and advisor to the Council. The TQM Coordinator plays a key role in developing and integrating the TQM Implementation Plan and aids in prioritizing suggestions for PATs based upon the Council's selected criteria. One responsibility is closely coordinating the training portion of the implementation plan with the company's training department. The TQM Coordinator also represents the organization in interface meetings involving other companies, divisions, sub-divisions, superior and subordinate organizations, as well as suppliers, on issues related to TQM. As a regular participant in Council meetings, he or she will also serve as secretariat.

Consulting services include a combination of in-house and hired consultants for routine and non-routine consulting assistance to the organization. Individuals within the organization who desire consulting services arrange these activities through the TQM Coordinator. It should be the eventual goal of the organization to have the majority of this support accomplished by in-house people. Consulting services provide one-on-one aid to the TQM Coordinator, the Council, and middle managers needing specific assistance in resolving TQM issues. The majority of in-house consultant time will be spent helping the PATs better understand the use of specific TQM tools and applying them to specific goals. In some ways, consulting services become an extension of formal training to PAT members. Remember, it is the responsibility of the PATs--not the consultants--to do the work.

The final Support Service is training. Because of the dynamics of this responsibility, early training will probably be accomplished by some form of contracted services with in-house assistance. This is due to the changing expertise of the trainers. The early phases require a heavy emphasis on concepts and principles. Later, training will shift, focusing on management and technical aspects. PAT members may need specialized training in small numbers, tailored to their task.

Let us summarize a few of the important points covered above. First, it is the responsibility of the TQM Coordinator to insure that training requirements flow from the corporate strategic plan, through the implementation plan, and become relevant, scheduled training classes. The organization training department interviews, selects, budgets, and schedules training through the TQM Coordinator.

Obstacles to Implementation

Resistance to change is inevitable, even when change offers improvement. This resistance consists of a mixture of real and perceived difficulties, not only within the workforce, but in management as well. Whether real or imagined, each resistance encountered must be met head-on with positive, enthusiastic support. Management's ability to overcome resistance early helps eliminate much of the fear and anxiety associated with change.

The best defense is a good offense! Anticipate resistance and establish mechanisms to overcome it before it creates a major problem. One of the best vehicles to accomplish this is awareness and orientation training for new and existing employees. You can also alleviate resistance through the organization's policy statement. If tied directly to employee recognition and rewards, the policy statement(s) will convey a positive message to both management and workforce. When developed properly and stated correctly, it can have workers saying to themselves, "Yes, I can also benefit from TQM by taking a chance." If the employee is convinced that he or she will gain something, you're on the right track. Employee benefits may include better working conditions, less frustration within the corporate structure, and possibly, financial reward.

The Corporate Council can contribute significantly to implementing TQM. Again, if done correctly, its mere presence conveys a message to the workforce: "We're behind you 100%." Here, the Council can pat someone on the back for merely suggesting a good idea. Further support is displayed by committing the corporate resources to charter new PATs. Last and most important, the Council removes barriers that make straight-forward solutions so difficult. The PAT members will have their hands full understanding, analyzing, and developing recommendations for the Council. In return, the Council must overcome the political umbrella which surrounds the problem being addressed by the PAT, across functional divisions of responsibility.

Other potential problems for Council consideration are included in Exhibit 19. Suggested solutions and approaches to resolving them are also provided. Executives may memorize these solutions or develop their own using their personal beliefs, or "English." You will hear or see these again in real life.

Consultants - Do You Need Them?

No doubt it has become apparent by now that I strongly recommend the use of consultants to help implement TQM. In fact, I can only think of one instance where TQM has successfully been implemented without some outside assistance. I am a consultant, and as you know, consultants recommend consultants much the way physicians recommend other physicians. Professional ethics, honesty, and courtesy dictate recommending specialists where nothing less

EXHIBIT 19.

Compilation of Some Likely Resistance-to-Change Issues and How They Might Be Overcome

Potential/Probable Issues	Suggested Solution or Approach
Management doesn't care.	We now realize the importance and value of our employees. Through TQM we wish to bring the workforce into the corporate decision-making process on issues affecting their careers and their jobs. Participative management is a foundational principle of TQM.
I don't believe TQM can work in our company.	The principles and tools of TQM have been successfully applied throughout hundreds of service and manufacturing organizations. Our goal is to learn the basics of TQM so we can begin creating success stories within our own company.
We do not have the resources to support. this initiative.	Yes, the implementation of TQM will cause all of us to sacrifice precious time. We all will be doing double duty, but this investment will yield great dividends. This initiative will actually save us time and money in the long term and will make us more competitive.
There is no continuity of leadership to support this initiative.	Yes, turnover at all levels is always a problem. If we demonstrate success early on and establish ourselves as being on track, no future staff will argue with our proven success, and we can continue the TQM process of improvement.

© Joseph R. Jablonski, 1990

than the best will do. Since your credibility as an executive is at stake, you will want to seek the best.

Consultants are specialists. The benefits from the application of their expertise to your specific situation will far exceed the cost to you. Their credibility and direct "hands-on" experience provide a faster and smoother transition toward Total Quality. Consultants have encountered and overcome the barriers and pitfalls of implementation; they possess detailed knowledge to minimize problems. For these reasons and many more, corporations routinely hire consultants. They are a bargain.

Credibility and Corporate Executives

Hiring a Consultant - What to Look For. Everyone has expectations. Depending on the talent you bring on board to help in TQM implementation, your consultant, "hired gun," guru, whatever you want to call him or her, should either reinforce or deny those expectations. A popular consultant response to the question, "When should I see results?" is, "It depends!" As it turns out, they're right. It does depend on many things. But, after spending some time within the company, consultants should be able to offer some suggestions as to what kinds of results you should expect to see and when.

I emphasize this point specifically because management does have expectations and if they do not receive a satisfactory answer from the consultant, they will maintain their own expectations as the standard. If it takes too long, or the magnitude of the first success is inconsistent with their expectations, bad things can happen. Typically, these "bad things" take the form of a breakdown in confidence between the corporate executive and the consultant. Worse yet, they can result in a changeover from one consultant to another. In that case, everyone loses.

Corporate executives should realize that changing consultants part way into the TQM implementation process is a big decision. It results in a substantial cost in both time and money on behalf of the corporation. More important, this action will be viewed as a discontinuity by the workforce and managers looking for a reason to circumvent this initiative. If executives lose credibility in this area, the costs can be great.

During discussions with prospective clients about implementing TQM, the subject of how long it will take surfaces early. I try to be as honest as possible, explaining that they can reasonably expect some visible results within six to nine months from the decision to implement.

Having committed myself, I feel obligated to provide the following caveats: (1) the results from the first few PATs should provide needed process improvements without the expectation of earth-shaking savings. That is because the first few gestures toward process improvement should be guaranteed successes, selected to give PAT members experience in using the basic principles and tools of TQM and boost their self-confidence, and (2) these early results are merely the tip of the iceberg--a vote of confidence from corporate executives to convey their resolve for the initiative. The transition of the corporate culture, that point where process improvement is a way of life, takes by some estimate seven to ten years. This is a long-term commitment.

Now let me qualify that remark, because I'm putting myself on the line. I can think of one example where it took more than a year to derive direct benefit from the initial training investment. In this specific instance the organization had not done its homework. A TQM guru was hired to begin mass training before the organization executives had even understood the importance of a coordinated and cohesive set of terminology. In addition, the consultant had not been previewed by a representative from either the Corporate Council or Training Department. As a result, he could not offer the audience hard-hitting relevant examples of how TQM could benefit them. It took the organization more than a year to recover from that catastrophe and get back on track. And unfortunately, the executives realized a significant setback and loss of credibility in the process.

So where do the six to nine months come from? Assuming Phase 0 is complete (a decision to proceed with implementation has been made) it will take at least a couple of months to accomplish initial corporate planning. Once begun, facilitators are recruited, and approximately four months later you should begin to see tangible results from their efforts. Six to nine months is ambitious, but I believe achievable under the right circumstances.

To facilitate a clear understanding, I must emphasize a key point. As corporate executives committing time and money to this initiative, you are entitled to have some expectations of positive results. The time to witness those results and their magnitude should be coordinated closely with the experience and expectation of your consultant. Make sure you are all in sync.

Chapter 6. Phase 2: Assessment

Phase 2, Assessment, includes four steps: Self- Evaluation, Organizational Assessment, Customer Survey, and Training Feedback. Exhibit 20 depicts these steps as milestones. All of these steps provide input for the TQM implementation process, feedback to management and the training department, and direct support for the company's strategic plan. Each step occurs more than once, with some repeated more frequently than others.

EXHIBIT 20.

Phase 2: Assessment

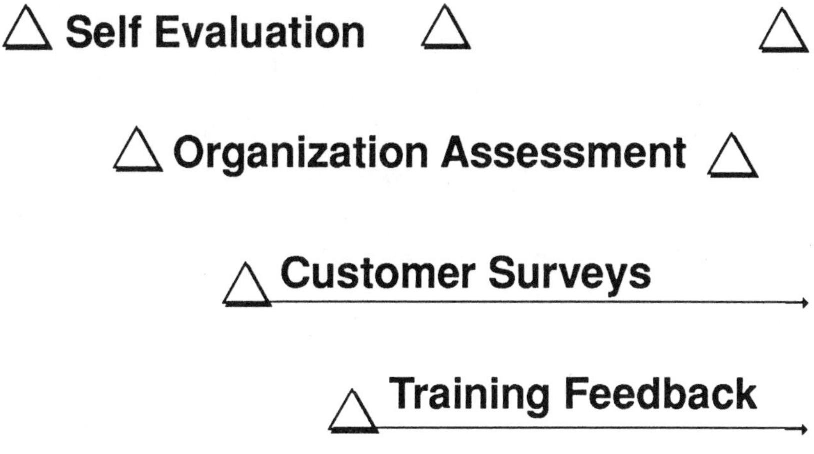

△ Self Evaluation △ △

△ Organization Assessment △

△ Customer Surveys

△ Training Feedback

© Joseph R. Jablonski, 1990

79

Self-Evaluation

First is Self-Evaluation. I like to use three basic surveys here. The version included in Exhibit 21 was developed by Philip Crosby, a guru in the U.S. Total Quality movement, and is titled "Where Is Your Organization in Terms of Quality?" An appropriate title. The self-evaluation is intended for use in facilitated meetings. Everyone receives a copy of the form, completes it, and calculates his/her own bottom-line score. It only takes a few minutes and yields profound results. The facilitator gathers the results by a show of hands and summarizes them on a flip chart. The objective in conducting this exercise is to have everyone ultimately agree that there is room for improvement in the way the company does business.

The Individual Survey Questionnaire in Exhibit 22 is used differently. A trained professional, usually a consultant who has no vested interest in the outcome, completes this form. It is important that individuals being interviewed accept the interviewer as a neutral party. The questions are intended to help management better understand employee perceptions of TQM and the role those perceptions will play in the TQM implementation process.

This survey should be completed by interviewing a significant number of employees across all levels within the organization including executive, management, and workforce personnel. If your company employs hundreds of people, ten percent would serve as an appropriate survey amount. If your company employs thousands, tens of thousands, or hundreds of thousands, a more reasonable sample would be in the range of 0.1 to 1.0 percent of its population. For larger organizations, these sampling figures should be applied to logical work units, such as divisions that operate stand-alone, separate from the rest of the organization. I mention that because a very large company may employ several hundred people at one location, such as a corporate headquarters, with other locations employing thousands or tens of thousands of people. An organization-wide survey would be accomplished at each site.

Employee perceptions reflected by the surveys will influence how you spend your training dollars. Anyone who listens to the radio or

EXHIBIT 21.

Where Is Your Organization in Terms of Quality?

Characteristics

Characteristics	That's us all the way	Some is true	We're not like that
1. Our services and/or products normally contain waivers, deviations, and other indications of not conforming to requirements.			
2. We have a "fix it" oriented field service and/or dealer organization.			
3. Our employees do not know what management wants from them concerning quality.			
4. Management does not know what the price of nonconformance really is.			
5. Management believes that quality is a problem caused by something other than management action.			
	5 Points	3 Points	1 Point

Point count condition 21-25 Critical.........Needs intensive care immediately.
16-20 Guarded......Needs life support system-hookup.
11-15 Resting.......Needs medication and attention.
6-10 Healing.......Needs regular checkup.
5 Whole........Needs counseling.

Reprinted with Permission, McGraw-Hill Book Company

EXHIBIT 22.

Sample Individual Survey Questionnaire

1. What does this company have to do to remain competitive in the future?

2. What types of initiatives are you currently addressing in your company to improve the way you do business?

3. What do you see as the reason for and benefit of TQM?

4. What are the most effective vehicles (formal and informal) to communicate information? (i.e. Top/Down, Bottom/Up)

5. If TQM is successful, what would it look like in your company? How could you measure it?

6. What are the corporate goals of your company? What is your role in the implementation of these goals?

7. What is your role in bringing company products and services to market? (Research and development, operation, administration, etc.)

8. How does your company differ from others in the same field? What are the strengths of your area? What are the weaknesses (things you'd like to change)?

9. What are the obstacles to implementing TQM?

10. What do you see as your role in the quality-improvement process?

11. What types of training and education would enhance your chances for success in this process?

12. Provide examples of the types of tools and techniques you have used in the implementation of TQM.

13. Describe the culture of your company (things people value, concerns, issues, beliefs).

14. How do you determine customer satisfaction?

15. Management commitment is a prerequisite for productivity/quality improvement. How will you demonstrate your commitment to TQM?

16. Who are your customers? (List them by name and company.)

© Joseph R. Jablonski, 1990

82

reads the newspaper knows of the quality movement sweeping the nation. If employees respond to this survey by saying, "This is great, now it's our turn to insure our competitive position and I can keep my job," you are on track and should feel good as an executive. If across the board your employees respond by saying, "What's all this got to do with me?" you have problems. So plan on spending more time early in training emphasizing the need for quality and the need to offer better products and services at a lower cost to remain competitive in today's marketplace and tomorrow's. Everyone must be sensitized to his or her role in making this a successful initiative and understand why it is being done in the first place.

A third self-evaluation tool I like to use is the Performax Systems International, Inc. Personal Profile System (C). It provides a means to better understand our own behavioral patterns and those of other people. It is used most effectively in the early stages of TQM, during team-building exercises. I like to employ it during the first training session for Process Action Teams (PATs).

Behavior patterns include the way we think, feel, and act in our day-to-day environment and how we respond to new demands and situations. An internationally-recognized expert on the subject of negotiating, Roger Dawson, uses this technique to better understand what turns on and what turns off the person he expects to do business with. Recognizing the four behavior patterns in the Performax System helps both in business endeavors and in making TQM a reality.

We refer to the four basic behavior profiles as D, I, S, and C. Each exhibit certain personality traits that are identifiable to the trained person. By understanding these personalities, you form a more effective TQM team. A high "D" profile person is characterized as a people mover, someone who is impatient. I am a high D. Someone with an "I" personality seeks recognition, is basically disorganized, and resists personal rejection. A person with an "S" personality is a cooperative group worker, possessive, and fearful of risk taking. Someone with a "C" personality is creative, fearful of rejection, and resistent to criticism of his/her ideas and work. Because profiles change when people experience stress, they can serve as indicators for times when others feel uncomfortable.

You may be asking yourself, "What does all this have to do with TQM and me?" It is important to note that all teams probably consist of a mix of individuals from each of the four personality types just described. Your understanding of these different personalities, their strengths and their fears will allow you to form a team more quickly and capitalize on individual strengths. It also moves you faster toward better process improvement solutions.

My focus in TQM over the last few years has been in the area of technical tools. I recently used the Performax Personality System, and it was an enlightening experience. I discovered that I possess a strong type-D personality. (Many engineers are D's.) A woman in our group stood up to describe the characteristics typical of D's. She began by saying they were movers and shakers, go-getters, decisive! I felt pretty good about myself. She then continued describing her perception of type-D's. All of a sudden it dawned on me that some of her remarks were not exactly complimentary. In fact, some were downright insulting. The terms "pushy" and "loud" stuck in my mind most. What hurt more was that she was right. Thus the moral of the story: the more you understand yourself and those around you, the better chance you have of getting along with others and working toward a common goal.

Having worked in both private industry and government for a number of years, I have attended more than my share of meetings. When introduced to someone for the first time, something surfaces early in the meeting that tells me whether we will get along famously, or whether something is just not right. TQM training helped me better understand the personality traits of others. Understanding traits that annoy me helps me work with people more effectively and ignore personality disconnects that previously hindered our business relationship. It makes good business sense to know about this.

The Personality Profile System by Performax is an excellent tool of TQM. For more information contact:

> Performax Systems International, Inc.
> Attn: Rich Meiss
> P.O. Box 59159 , Minneapolis, MN 55459-8247
> (612) 449-2856

Organizational Assessment

Organizational Assessment provides an important mechanism for understanding yourself, your organization as a corporate entity, and its members. It essentially evaluates the current state of an organization, assesses a multitude of factors, and can lead to positive, action-oriented recommendations for improvement. Factors that contribute to the development of these recommendations include the organization's "vision" of where it wants to be, as well as the customers' expectations. The organizational assessment process can account for numerous factors, measuring and quantifying variables that some considered unmeasurable. An individual's beliefs serve as an example.

One aspect of the organization on which the assessment can focus is organizational culture (*Organization Culture Inventory Leader's Guide*, Cooke, 1989). Culture can be described as the thoughts, behavior, and beliefs that members of an organization have in common. In attempting to measure and apply the concept, it is useful to think of culture in terms of the shared values and beliefs that guide the way organization members interact with one another and approach their work. Literature provides many definitions of culture, but all tend to emphasize certain things: (1) culture is something shared by members of an organization; (2) values-- "what is important"--and beliefs -- "how things work" -- are central components of culture; and (3) culture encompasses norms and expectations that influence the way members of the organization think and behave (Cooke and Rousseau, 1988). Assessing an organization's culture can be accomplished via personal interviews with employees, a walk through of an organization, a review of employee performance, and the administration of surveys. One such survey is the *Organizational Culture Inventory* or OCI ™ (Cooke and Lafferty, 1989).

The results obtained from surveys such as the OCI can indicate whether an organization has a relatively strong culture (high consensus among respondents regarding norms or values), a weak culture, or no culture at all (no consensus among respondents). The results can also show that the prevailing culture differs substantially from the values and norms members believe would contribute to organizational effectiveness. For example, employees might perceive that they are expected to simply "follow orders and not get involved," but that "participation in decision making" is critical for achieving excellence in quality. If this were the case, such findings could explain low motivation, unmet goals, members' dissatisfaction with the system and, interestingly, the reasons behind members' perception of the organizational climate. Information of this type, otherwise unavailable to consultants and their clients, provides an important vehicle for organizational change and development. Therein lies its value in TQM.

After identifying disconnects or "gaps" between the organization's present culture and the desired culture, relevant recommendations to support TQM can be made to corporate executives. These insights provide both the corporate leader and consultant with tangible, measurable changes possible in the organization's way of doing business to support its vision more effectively. The results of an OCI play a key role in developing the corporate strategic plan and provide direct input for the training plan. Later in Chapter 7 we will see the important role training plays in making TQM happen.

The survey I like, *The Organizational Culture Inventory* (OCI), is offered by Human Synergistics™ of Plymouth, Michigan. Through a set of 120 statements the OCI measures twelve different cultural styles or, more specifically, twelve sets of behavioral norms and expectations that might exist in an organization. These statements measure the extent to which organizational norms support and encourage Dependent, Power-Oriented, Competitive, Achievement, and eight other behavioral styles. Based on their responses to these items, individual members can develop a profile of their impressions of the organization's culture, using the Organizational Culture Profile (OCP) shown in Exhibit 23. This normed profile allows them to compare their responses to those of approximately 4,000 members of other organizations. Understanding the individual member's impressions of norms and expectations is an important step toward developing a picture of section, department, division, or any corporate subculture.

EXHIBIT 23.

Organizational Culture Inventory Circumplex

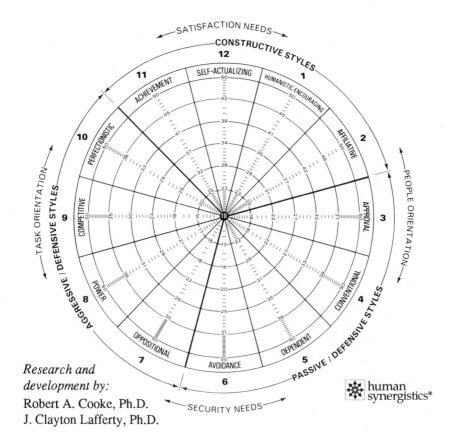

Research and
development by:
Robert A. Cooke, Ph.D.
J. Clayton Lafferty, Ph.D.

human
synergistics®

Averages may be taken across all respondents (along all twelve categories) and plotted the very same way to yield a composite picture of the organization's sub-units, such as sections, divisions, etc. Recent studies have shown that the "shape" of the resultant profile relates to such outcomes as the perceived quality of products and services and the supportiveness of the organization's culture to quality.

Human Synergistics also offers a multitude of different products--from diagnostic instruments, such as the <u>OCI</u> and the *Life Styles Inventory* ™ to team-building simulations, such as *Desert Survival* and the *Project Planning Situation*. What makes these products exceptional is the extensive research and testing behind them. They have stood the test of time and are backed by reliable statistical documentation; therefore, they can help your organization identify its relative strengths and opportunities for improvement. If you believe by now that the Organizational Assessment is a big job, requiring skilled, professional help, then I have been successful. Finding the tools necessary to evaluate your company is a complicated task. For more information on the products and services available through Human Synergistics contact:

> Human Synergistics, Inc.
> 39819 Plymouth Rd.
> Plymouth, MI 48170
> (313) 459-1030

Customer Survey

The customer survey provides an important assessment tool. It presents an opportunity to convey your concern for customer satisfaction and your appreciation for their business. How many times have you lost valued customers, only to discover later that some small detail or minor price difference caused them to move to a competitor? The customer survey helps determine exactly what your customer expects from your organization.

Exhibit 24 provides an example of a customer survey. While this survey should be tailored to your particular needs, it should always obtain certain basic information such as, "What are we doing right?" and "What can we improve upon?" In contrast to the Organizational Culture Inventory described above, you probably cannot expect your customer to spend a lot of time completing it. Therefore, it behooves you to use innovative approaches to gather this information. One option involves asking these questions during a regular business meeting, either in person or over the telephone. You do not have to let your customers know you are querying them. If deficiencies in your performance surface during the discussion, let them know you are taking positive steps to correct them. Keep the customers informed of your progress, to show you are interested in their concerns and interested in retaining them as valued customers.

EXHIBIT 24.

Sample Customer Survey

A Measure of Customer Satisfaction
Mackay Envelope Corporation

Prepared by Keller, Rosen and Associates

Directions: After each question, please write the number corresponding to the answer that best reflects your opinion. If a question does not apply to your area of responsibility, write Not Applicable (N/A).

Very Dissatisfied			Very Satisfied		Not Applicable
1	2	3	4	5	N/A

1. **How satisfied are you with the following aspects of ENVELOPES you purchase from Mackay Envelope?**

   a. Sufficient styles and types to meet your envelope needs _____

   b. Promptness in preparing quotations _____

   c. Responsiveness in attending to your special requests _____

   d. Competitive pricing _____

   e. Artwork preparation _____

   f. Quality of envelope construction _____

   g. Envelope performance on your inserting equipment _____

   h. Quality of printing _____

   i. Overall quality of products _____

2. **How satisfied are you with the following INTERPERSONAL FACTORS related to Mackay Envelope SALES REPRESENTATIVES?**

   a. Making effective use of the time spent with you _____

   b. Calling on your account often enough _____

   c. Returning phone calls promptly _____

   d. Friendliness and courtesy _____

   e. Reliability _____

   f. Developing a long-term relationship with you _____

   g. Overall performance _____

EXHIBIT 24. (Cont.)

Sample Customer Survey

A Measure of Customer Satisfaction
Mackay Envelope Corporation   *Page 2*

3. **How satisfied are you with the following TECHNICAL FACTORS related to Mackay Envelope SALES REPRESENTATIVES?**

   a. Understanding your business and envelope needs   _____

   b. Knowledge of Mackay Envelope products and services   _____

   c. Knowledge of current postal requirements   _____

   d. Making cost-effective recommendations   _____

   e. Overall technical competence   _____

4. **How satisfied are you with Mackay Envelope's BUSINESS POLICIES AND PROCEDURES?**

   a. Availability of credit   _____

   b. Accuracy of invoices   _____

   c. Timeliness of invoices   _____

   d. Responsiveness to billing inquiries   _____

5. **How satisfied are you with DELIVERY of the envelopes you purchase from Mackay Envelope?**

   a. Availability of standard envelopes/in stock   _____

   b. Length of time between placing an order and delivery   _____

   c. Meeting agreed-upon delivery schedules   _____

   d. Emergency service/filling rush orders   _____

   e. Notification of shipping delay, if necessary   _____

   f. Clarity of container labeling   _____

   g. Physical condition of the shipment on arrival   _____

   h. Correctness of order as delivered   _____

   i. Overall delivery performance   _____

EXHIBIT 24. (Cont.)

Sample Customer Survey

A Measure of Customer Satisfaction
Mackay Envelope Corporation   *Page 3*

6. **How satisfied are you with performance when you call Mackay Envelope to PLACE AN ORDER or for CUSTOMER SERVICE?**

   a. Speed of phone answering at Mackay Envelope   _____

   b. Ease of reaching the appropriate person by phone   _____

   c. Efficiency of Mackay Envelope telephone system   _____

   d. Promptness in returning phone calls   _____

   e. Promptness in responding to your requests   _____

   f. Courtesy and friendliness   _____

   g. Accuracy of orders   _____

   h. Overall ease of placing an order   _____

   i. Availability of order status information   _____

   j. Availability of delivery date information   _____

   k. Understanding the nature of the problem to be solved _____

   l. Overall technical competence   _____

   m. Overall performance   _____

7. **Please indicate your OVERALL PERCEPTIONS of Mackay Envelope.**

   a. Mackay is innovative in the envelopes it designs to
       meet customer requirements   _____

   b. Mackay meets our needs for customer-
       designed envelopes   _____

   c. Mackay provides high-quality printing   _____

   d. Mackay has an excellent reputation for providing high-
       quality products and services   _____

   e. Mackay consistently achieves a high level
       of customer satisfaction   _____

   f. Mackay pricing is competitive   _____

Question 7 continued on next page.

91

EXHIBIT 24. (Cont.)

Sample Customer Survey

A Measure of Customer Satisfaction
Mackay Envelope Corporation   *Page 4*

---

   g. Mackay business practices make it easy
      for me as a customer   _____

   h. Mackay keeps the promises it makes to customers   _____

   i. I would recommend Mackay as a supplier to
      others with envelope needs similar to mine   _____

**8a.   If you have had experience with other envelope manufacturers,
please rate Mackay Envelope compared to them.**

   a. Envelope quality   _____

   b. Printing quality   _____

   c. Pricing   _____

   d. Delivery performance   _____

   e. Responsiveness to requests for quotes   _____

   f. Availability of order status information   _____

   g. Range of envelopes available   _____

   h. Innovation and creativity   _____

   i. Sales rep effectiveness   _____

   j. Customer service/ordering by phone   _____

   k. Overall reputation   _____

**8b.   Please write the name of the envelope supplier who, in your opinion,
offers the best overall performance in terms of product, service,
price, and business support programs.**

EXHIBIT 24. (Cont.)

Sample Customer Survey

A Measure of Customer Satisfaction
Mackay Envelope Corporation

9. Which three of the following do you consider the MOST IMPORTANT FACTORS when selecting an envelope manufacturer? (Even if other factors are also important, please mark only the most important three.)

   a. Envelope quality _____

   b. Printing quality _____

   c. Pricing _____

   d. Delivery performance _____

   e. Responsiveness to requests for quotes _____

   f. Availability of order status information _____

   g. Range of envelopes available _____

   h. Innovation and creativity _____

   i. Sales rep effectiveness _____

   j. Customer Service/ordering by phone _____

   k. Overall reputation _____

   i. Other _____ _____

10. Please use the space below to provide comments or suggestions about how Mackay Envelope could increase your satisfaction with its products and services.

11. Overall, are you more or less likely to do business with Mackay Envelope today than you were in the past?

   1. Less likely _____

   2. More likely _____

   3. Anticipate no change _____

   4. Unsure _____

Mackay Envelope management will read all customer comments. If you would like your comments identified, please sign below. Without your signed permission, your comments will be used anonymously.

_____

Signature
Thank you for taking the time to help us serve you better.

You can conduct a customer survey anywhere in the TQM improvement process. However it should be conducted and the results compiled, before the Corporate Council makes its decision on which implementation strategy to employ. At this point the Council determines the criteria for selecting problems for resolution, and PATs are formed. Customer feedback, a crucial factor, may greatly influence the council's selection of a strategy.

Training Feedback

Training feedback comprises the fourth and final step of the assessment phase. By the time you receive your first training survey, the organization's training department will have invested a lot of time in selecting and scheduling training. This is your first opportunity to view the perceptions of the training attendees and to evaluate the impact your investment has had on the bottom line.

Exhibit 25 shows a sample training survey. Although it is only an example, like the customer survey, it should include two basic questions: "How did we do?" and "How can we improve?" If initial training for managers or the workforce has not been effective, you'll need time to make the necessary course adjustments using these survey results. Obtaining surveys from each training session should be routine, with the results being compiled and summarized by the training department and reviewed by both the training department representative and the TQM Coordinator. The results of these surveys should also be brought to the attention of the Council, since it represents one of the largest financial commitments of the decision to proceed into implementation.

Training Results and the Bottom Line

People frequently overlook the relationship between training and the bottom line. Because training comprises a large part of your TQM budget, we need to address this subject.

I've described many things to this point--corporate goals, self-evaluation, feedback--and many more things that contribute support to your corporate strategic plan. In order to meet corporate goals, employees must have sufficient knowledge, skills, and

EXHIBIT 25.

Sample Training Survey

WORKSHOP CRITIQUE SHEET

Course:_____ Dates:_____

Instructor:_____

| | Please Circle One | | | |
	EXCELLENT	GOOD	FAIR	POOR
1. COVERAGE OF SUBJECT MATTER	A	B	C	D
2. ORGANIZATION OF SUBJECT MATTER	A	B	C	D
3. PRESENTATION OF SUBJECT MATTER	A	B	C	D
4. EXERCISES USED FOR SUBJECT MATTER	A	B	C	D
5. SUITABILITY OF INSTRUCTIONAL MATERIAL	A	B	C	D
6. LEVEL OF DIFFICULTY	A	B	C	D
7. LENGTH OF COURSE	A	B	C	D
8. EFFECTIVENESS OF INSTRUCTOR	A	B	C	D
9. APPLICABILITY OF SUBJECT MATTER TO THE JOB	A	B	C	D

10. RECOMMENDATION TO CO-WORKERS (Circle one from below)

    HIGHLY RECOMMEND   NOT RECOMMEND   RECOMMENDED

COMMENTS ON STRONG POINTS OF COURSE:
_____
_____

COMMENTS ON WEAK POINTS OF COURSE:
_____
_____

WHAT WILL YOU DO DIFFERENTLY AS A RESULT OF HAVING ATTENDED
THIS TRAINING SESSION?_____
_____
_____

SUGGESTED IMPROVEMENTS:_____
_____
_____

GENERAL COMMENTS ON COURSE:_____
_____
_____

© Joseph R. Jablonski, 1990

attitudes to perform. Hence they must be trained. A well-designed strategic plan yields measurable goals. Since we measure employee performance in meeting these goals, the results of training must be measurable.

Providing good training requires a four-level evaluation process: (1) Reaction—were the trainees satisfied with the program? (2) Learning—what facts, techniques, skills or attitudes did the trainees understand and absorb? (3) Behavior—did the program change the trainees' behavior in a way that improves on-the-job performance? (4) Results—did the program produce the desired results?

Employee reaction to training, learning, and behavior is reflected to varying degrees in the Sample Training Survey form shown in Exhibit 25. The fourth element, results, presents a more difficult challenge. Here tangible results from training are provided to the Corporate Council as feedback, confirming that the training investment is paying off. On-Target training offers this important link to the bottom line using its own structured evaluation system.

First, the organization's training program is assessed to determine a proper fit. Have the objectives been clearly defined? How will value to the organization be assessed? Next, the evaluation instrument is designed. One size does not fit all. Finally, the individuals who will use the evaluation instrument must realize how to derive the greatest benefit from it. Managers learn to convey expectations and to provide a foundation for follow-up. They identify and eliminate barriers that can sabotage training. Rewards and reinforcement for performance are established, and training needs and results are communicated to the training department. For more information on how to relate training results to your bottom line, contact:

> Jane Holcomb, Ph.D.
> On-Target Training
> 7805 W. 80th Street
> Playa del Ray, CA 90293
> (213) 821-7624

To recap, various types of surveys, questionnaires, and interviews necessary to implement TQM have been discussed. Their timing in the TQM Implementation Process is merely suggested. Certain types of assessments lend themselves to routine, scheduled use by the organization. One-time use of these assessment vehicles only benchmarks the existing organization. Reuse of the same or similar questionnaire at some time later (perhaps one year) will indicate a clear trend in performance. The TQM Coordinator should maintain training statistics and track progress, possibly using some simple tools of TQM. Later, when I describe problem-solving skills in Chapter 7, you will better understand the significance of bench-marking and trending.

Chapter 7. Phase 3:
Implementation

Overview

We have finally arrived! After Preparation, Planning and Assessment, we reach that point where we will see a return on our investment of time and money. This is Phase 3, Implementation.

Here, the organization's facilitators are selected and trained, a TQM library is put in place, managers and workforce personnel are trained, PATs are put in place and if all goes well, you begin to see results. Exhibit 26 summarizes the steps necessary to accomplish implementation. Each step is later described in detail.

Organization Facilitators

Step 1 involves selection of the organization's facilitators. These important people will maintain high-visibility positions within the organization as an extension of the TQM Coordinator. The Facilitator will serve in the consulting and training role as part of Support Services described in Chapter 5, Forming the Team. Like the TQM Coordinator, these individuals should be selected with great care.

After the initial training, these in-house facilitators will begin the transition away from a consultant-driven implementation process. Their first few sessions to train management and workforce personnel will be co-facilitated with the aid of the consultant, who fields the difficult questions and helps smooth over the rough spots. At this stage, both the facilitators and the "hired guns" are really earning their pay--and then some. Organization Facilitators should be selected using similar standards to those for the TQM Coordinator. After taking the helm in training, they will become the in-house experts, assuming increased responsibilities in interpersonal and problem-solving skills. Facilitators should represent all levels within the organization, including workforce, management, and executive personnel. They must be volunteers with credibility and a strong commitment to the organization's development. You will make a substantial investment in these people; capitalize on that.

The Organization Facilitators receive the same training as the TQM Coordinator: a two-week, intensive training evolution exposing each Facilitator to a broad-based training experience. This includes a mix of the principles, concepts, and tools of TQM.

EXHIBIT 26.

Phase 3: Implementation

△ Select Organization Facilitators

△ Train Facilitators

△ EstablishTQM Library

△ Train Managers

△ Train Workforce

△ PATs Functioning

☆ 1st Success Story

© Joseph R. Jablonski

100

As the training proceeds, "specialists" emerge. After completing the training, each person begins to identify with those topics he or she feels most comfortable with. Some will gravitate toward the more technical tools, such as control charts. Others may focus on presentation skills or conducting personality profile exercises. No matter. The TQM Coordinator will schedule organization personnel, using the strengths and specialized skills of each. Everyone can contribute.

Next it is timely to create a TQM library. It should contain relevant texts, periodicals, case studies, audio and video tapes. Content selection should be based upon two considerations. (1) It should include relevant material to aid in the TQM training process, and (2) it should serve as a ready resource to support the organization's facilitators, PATs, and other interested parties. Appendix A provides convenient sources for this type of information.

Management and Workforce Training

Steps 4 and 5 involve training management and workforce personnel. This area presents problems for many companies. Group or large-scale training should begin only after the completion of necessary planning, the selection of terminology you will use, and the propagation of executive momentum throughout the organization. If you follow this approach, you can safely proceed on solid footing.

Exhibit 27 outlines a road map for the kinds of training each employee will receive. I divide training into three basic categories: (1) Awareness Training, (2) Orientation Training, and (3) Skills Training. Like the pieces of a puzzle, each plays a specific role, critical to transitioning all employees toward Total Quality. The most valuable aspect of my training approach is timing. Each session provides employees with enough information so they may digest it, discover which facets of TQM they agree with, and identify those parts of TQM they simply do not believe. That's fine. A later training session will address these concerns. All issues are real, and they are dealt with directly in open forums.

EXHIBIT 27.

Corporate-Wide Training to Support
TQM Implementation

Awareness

❑ What is TQM?
❑ How can it help us?
❑ Others who have succeeded

Orientation

❑ What is our plan?
❑ What is my role?
❑ What will be expected of me?

Skills

❑ PAT
❑ Team Building
❑ Customer Service
❑ Taguchi Methods

© Joseph R. Jablonski, 1990

Awareness training is the first exposure your people will have in TQM. This pivotal introduction plants the seed that TQM is good and will benefit them. Most important, it should be brief--fifty minutes maximum. This presentation should be polished, well-organized, and prepared to address basic concepts: (1) What is Total Quality Management?, (2) Who has benefited?, and (3) How can it help you? If the necessity of TQM is not yet apparent, address an additional point describing the need for quality as a survival mechanism for the company (and the country) in order to compete and prosper in the existing world economy. The need for this additional point becomes evident after compiling results from the self-evaluation in Phase 2. Everyone must believe that a need to improve the way he does business exists, and that TQM is a proven vehicle for accomplishing that goal.

Orientation Training will be longer--about three to four hours. Here, each employee learns of the company's strategic plan to make Total Quality a way of life. All of the time, planning, and pain that have been invested thus far are unveiled for all to see. To a corporate executive, this represents reward time. As such, a senior person from within the company should play a key role in the presentation. Beyond discovering the magnitude of the changes taking place, each employee should understand a handful of key points. (1) There is top-level commitment. They know that because you are present, in the flesh, telling them. (2) Everyone in the organization will be affected in a positive fashion. If something about your job causes you dissatisfaction, now is the time to improve it. (3) Everyone contributes in this process. Employees who have not already volunteered to become a facilitator should know they will have many other opportunities to participate. (4) Finally, they receive a schedule of what can be expected and when. There will be no surprises, and everyone will know what is happening. They will be kept abreast of chartered PATs and recognized for their progress and contributions toward making TQM a reality.

Specific skills training comprises the third element in the training process. We've already discussed in detail the generic training presented to everyone in the company. Here, I will describe specific training apportioned based upon needs. This can include leadership training, presentation skills training, telephone answering skills, etc. Sound familiar? That's right, much of the skills training represents a continuation of the already planned and budgeted training initiatives. The difference is that TQM will relate it to the organization's corporate strategic plan, based upon a determination of needs. These needs become apparent as opportunities for improvement surface during the Assessment Phase.

I recently presented a series of Awareness Training sessions to a local organization in the Albuquerque area. Managers were anxious to implement TQM, streamline processes, and change the world. Although they focused upon using rather sophisticated technical tools of TQM, it was evident that they could achieve great returns in the short-term by applying simpler techniques. For example, I realized (as did probably everyone who tried to call them) that their telephone skills were abysmal. It was common-place for the telephone to ring five and sometimes ten times before someone would answer it. I mention this because all too often, executives and managers pursue complex solutions to commonplace problems and in doing so, overlook the basics. Yes, much of the training your people obtain through TQM reemphasizes the basics: team building, group dynamics, and of course, let's not overlook telephone techniques.

Process Action Team Training

Probably the most obvious, focused, TQM training that your company will realize is Process Action Team (PAT) training. This training serves as the "meat and potatoes" component of your entire TQM effort. It yields the results--the success stories--you have been looking for. PAT training consists of the five basic parts described in Exhibit 28: (1) Introduction and Overview, (2) Information Gathering, (3) Analysis and Interpretation, (4) Packaging and Presentation, and (5) Follow-up. The sequencing and timing of these training events are crucial.

Just as timing is vital in presenting Awareness and Orientation Training to all employees, the timing of each component of PAT training is also important. Each component should give trainees just enough information to do something. That means, provide people enough skills training so they can go forth and practice these skills with some mechanism in place for addressing questions and refining concepts for application to their specific process. Each PAT and PAT member should have access to a specialist who addresses specific problems as they arise. The TQM Coordinator will make this support available; it consists of a mix of in-house and hired consultants. In the course of training, PAT members learn both technical and non-technical tools. They will apply these tools using a structured problem-solving approach.

Shewhart Cycle

One model for problem solving, or continuous process improvement, is the Shewhart Cycle, shown in Exhibit 29. It includes four

EXHIBIT 28.

Skills Training to Support TQM Implementation

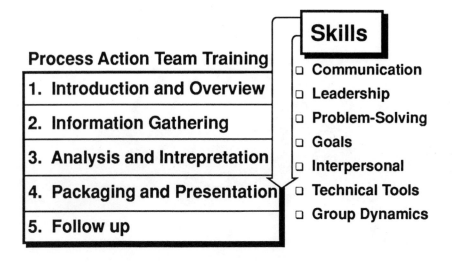

Process Action Team Training	Skills
1. Introduction and Overview	❑ Communication
2. Information Gathering	❑ Leadership
3. Analysis and Intrepretation	❑ Problem-Solving
4. Packaging and Presentation	❑ Goals
5. Follow up	❑ Interpersonal
	❑ Technical Tools
	❑ Group Dynamics

quadrants--four parts to improve processes: Plan (P), Do (D), Check (C), and Act (A).

P represents the beginning, early planning. Using the tools of TQM to identify an opportunity for process improvement, we define the problem, identify the customer, and understand what quality characteristic is important for the process under study. D, or Do, comes next. Here we develop solutions to improve the process. When one solution is approved, we prepare a schedule and resource estimates to implement the process improvement. Employees are trained to smooth the transition to the new, improved process.

Next is Check, or C. After implementing the new process we must identify what actually happened. During P and D, we developed expectations as to how the process would perform after changes were approved and implemented. Now we measure the same quality characteristics and compare them against the original, or benchmarked, values.

EXHIBIT 29.

The Shewhart Cycle

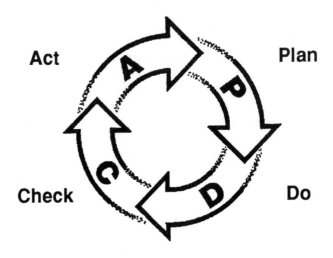

Act · Plan · Check · Do

A P C D

© Joseph R. Jablonski, 1990

Last is Act, or A. Here, we incorporate successful process improvements as a work standard. This success is applied to other, similar processes, and we address the question, ''What should we do next?'' This presents the first opportunity to communicate success to subordinate organizations and suppliers.

Five Parts of PAT Training

During the first part of PAT Training, Introduction and Overview, employees receive training in small groups. Each group consists of four to eight individuals, and each team will be trained to address a specific process identified for improvement by the Corporate Council. These processes may have been selected in several ways. They may have resulted from a brainstorming session with corporate executives, a problem that surfaced during the Organizational Assessment, or a customer complaint. I cannot overemphasize the importance of training each group as a team. PAT training provides the initial occasion for creating that bond which will develop between cross-functional entities within your company. Forming this team allows everyone to get special treatment and play a key role in making something positive happen. Teamwork allows team members to fulfill their potential.

The skills taught during Introduction & Overview include team building, brainstorming, interpersonal, group dynamics, and understanding processes. Participants learn basic skills that allow them to work together more effectively. The Performax Personality System provides a tool for assessing personality strengths and weaknesses. Participants learn how to understand processes. Flow charting serves as the most fundamental means for accomplishing this goal. This powerful tool graphically depicts all of the steps, activities, and operations necessary to accomplish a goal. It is a simple technique, easily understood by people with very diverse experience and educational backgrounds. As a result of my training, one person, whom I will call Paul, used flowcharts to communicate how the pieces of a software project could be assembled over time to yield a tremendous capability in the long term, while offering the customer smaller incremental improvements in capability in the short term. He got the job! After completing Part One of PAT training, participants will be armed to work toward process improvement as a team, flow charting their process.

After completing their flow charts, the PATs return to the classroom for the second part of their training--Information Gathering. Here, they learn to use the flow chart symbols to brainstorm opportunities for information that would allow them to quantify the performance of the existing process and identify numerical goals for process improvement. In sessions like this, specialized expertise of each individual comes to light. Clearly, some individuals will shine, having the groups arrive at a list of priorities, brainstormed alternatives. Others will feel more comfortable describing data availability, explaining how that information can most easily be obtained, and identifying ways to compile this information for later use. Everyone can play this role. Upon completing Part 2 of PAT training, each team will be able to gather and summarize the researched information in preparation for the next training session.

Part 3 of PAT training is Analysis and Interpretation. Here, the information gathered since the last training session is reviewed.

Participants learn skills that allow them to extract usable information from their data, while applying some basic tools of TQM. These might include a simple tubular compilation of the data, a Pareto Diagram, a control chart, or any number of tools made available to the new problem-solving professionals. These basic tools will be used in preparation for Part 4 of PAT training. Oftentimes the information is presented several different ways for Part 4 training, to develop the best, most concise method for presentation to the Corporate Council.

Part 4, Packaging and Presentation, is where the labors of PAT members come to fruition. Here, the results of analysis and interpretation are reviewed, the information summarizing the best efforts documented for review by the TQM Coordinator, and a brief summary of your recommendations prepared for presentation during the next Corporate Council meeting. Remember, this presentation is a sales pitch; this section of PAT training prepares participants to deliver it. Hence, the training includes practicing the presentation with hand-drawn overhead transparencies or a flip chart. When PATs leave this forum, they are ready to "sell" their ideas. Aside from any visual or graphic support, all is done. They are ready. Exhibit 30 includes a sample PAT report outline. I like to keep its length at ten pages or less, plus data and analysis charts. When the PAT disbands, the TQM Coordinator keeps this report so others with similar, or related, processes can benefit from it in the future.

Executive Reinforcement at the Right Time

Ok, you have a PAT understanding a process, analyzing data--everything seems to be going well and then it strikes--Failure! What happened? What escaped you? Here we observe a common phenomenon. I call it the attitude cycle, shown in Exhibit 31, and it plays an important role in management's ability to maintain momentum in the TQM initiative. As time goes by, PATs experience certain things as they move from the left of the attitude cycle to the right. How you, as an executive, respond to certain characteristics midway through this cycle directly influences whether a particular PAT succeeds or fails. Let's look at an example.

EXHIBIT 30.

Sample Process Action Team Report Outline

Cover

I. OVERVIEW

A. Executive Statement

B. Team Purpose

    1. To make recommendations based on data collected and analyzed

    2. To ask for concurrence from Corporate Council

    3. To continue to review and improve

II. INTRODUCTION (Background)

A. Brief History

B. Process Action Team Members

C. PAT Objectives

III. PROCESS SELECTION

A. Selection Process

    1. Brainstorming

    2. Flow Chart

    3. Cause & Effect Diagram

B. Project Description

IV. PROJECT IMPLEMENTATION

A. What Data Collected?

B. Where Data Collected?

C. When Data Collected?

D. How Data Collected?

E. Who Collected the Data?

V. ANALYSIS AND RECOMMENDATIONS

A. Process Changes

B. Cost Savings

VI. CONTINUING IMPROVEMENTS

A. PAT Schedule

B. PAT Recommendations

C. PAT Follow-up

© Joseph R. Jablonski, 1990

109

EXHIBIT 31.

Maintaining Momentum

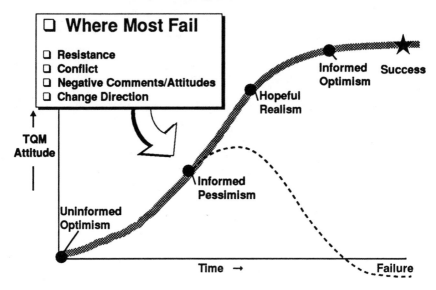

© Joseph R. Jablonski, 1990

It's the first day of class. A number of your people are in a room, eagerly awaiting their introductory session on PAT training. As the first hour leads to the daily wrap-up, everyone is enthusiastic, ready to do great things. They are pumped up. I call it "Uninformed Optimism." Yes, the training adequately prepares them for the tasks at hand, but other forces are at work--forces that will determine the ultimate success or failure of their efforts.

When people complete their first training session, they will begin to understand their process, usually through flow charting. They will be the first to gain this insight. And because they are the first, their challenge exceeds that of future PATs. When they solicit support and show enthusiasm for the process, they will probably encounter many disbelievers. At that stage, the PATs reach a mode I call "Informed Pessimism." Others have taken the wind out of their sails; they begin to believe that corporate change is too difficult, maybe even impossible. They require reinforcement, and that is where you come in. Your visible support, your presence in PAT coordination meetings, your verbal reinforcement when greeting these special people in the halls, help them overcome the slump and press on to success.

If you feel you are too busy, or the task too basic for someone of your stature, the PAT will undoubtedly fail. As Exhibit 31 shows, failure takes you below where you had been before as a company in your "TQM Attitude." Can this really be true? Can spending the time and money to train people actually result in a worse situation? It can.

In Chapter 3, I describe management commitment. The most valuable commodity you have to offer your PAT members is time. They want to know who is driving the boat and they want to "see" visible evidence of that support. Applying your precious time to these critical instances is essential and will propel your people through "Hopeful Realism," "Informed Optimism," and eventually lead to success. Everyone on the PAT needs your support at key points in the process of improvement. Eventually, previous PAT members will supply this aid, but in the early stages, your support is invaluable and your rewards immeasurable.

First Success Story

Part 5, Follow-up, is reward time. Here experienced PAT members brief new PAT members during the early stages of their training. In this rewarding experience, newcomers to TQM receive real-world feedback from their peers on the challenges and accomplishments encountered only months before. Even not-so-pleasant experiences are valuable, as everyone in the room learns how to overcome an adverse situation that may arise again. Using good project management practices, the PAT anticipates results after a certain period of time. We base the measure of success upon how close the PATs come to meeting the performance parameter goal they themselves had developed. Another measure, probably more important, is the learning experience taking place. Although we want success stories early on, we also need an education and an understanding of the pitfalls encountered and how to overcome such adversity. Yes, the excellent companies celebrate failure almost as much as they celebrate success. In doing so, they remove employees' hesitation about venturing into the unknown. Whether successful or not, PAT members should know they have the full support of the Corporate Council and the encouragement to participate in the future, regardless of the past. We all have to learn. The instructor, as an added benefit, advertises him or herself as an expert in the field and readily helps others as an in-house consultant. It is a special experience.

How Much Training Is Required?

At this point, you might be thinking, "Gee, this seems like a lot of training, what's all this going to cost?" Chapter 10 addresses the cost aspect. For now, it is important to review the magnitude of training realized by each level within the organization. You'll find these results summarized in Exhibit 32. While the specifics differ for each company, I believe the allocation of training to be widely applicable. As you can see, the training process involves everyone.

EXHIBIT 32.

Estimated Initial Training Requirements Necessary to Implement TQM

Type of Training

Layer within Organization	Principles & Concepts	Management Overview	Technical Overview	Specific Skills
Executive	2	2	.5	Days - Weeks
Management	1.5	1.5	.5	Days - Weeks
Workforce	1	.5	.5	Days - Weeks

* All Estimates are Measured in Days of Training.

© Joseph R. Jablonski, 1990

Awareness and Orientation training represents only a small fraction of the training each company employee will accomplish. Note the majority of the time, hence the majority of training resources, is allocated to specific skills training. Again, this emphasizes the need for analyzing and interpreting the results from the Assessment Phase to spend dollars most effectively. Training is a key element in making TQM work. Everyone in the company must realize that his turn will come in the training process, and that he will be expected to contribute.

Tools to Aid in Process Improvement

To date, most software packages that aid in process improvement have been written for the technocrat. Difficult to use and unforgiving for the user, they require an extensive background in statistics. This need not be the case.

Recent developments by a software firm in Albuquerque, New Mexico, have resulted in an easy-to-use, user-friendly, software program to aid PAT participants, called "The Tools of Total Quality Management." Some examples of its capabilities are described below.

Exhibit 33 depicts a simple Cause and Effect (C&E) diagram through an administrative example. It allows the PAT, through brainstorming, to identify the events or causes that result in an undesirable outcome. In this example the effect, to the right of the diagram, is "meetings take too long." Typically we focus our attention on this outcome and pay little attention to its cause. Hence, the need for the structured approach to problem solving we discussed earlier. TQM teaches us to identify the cause of this undesirable outcome so we can resolve it.

The administrative example described above was created from a table completed by a PAT member. Basic information, such as title and effect, is completed for the C&E diagram. The table summarizes such items as main-cause categories, brainstormed causes, as well as an additional column for comments. These comments provide supplemental documentation for the PAT member presenting a status report to the Corporate Council. Information is easy to enter

EXHIBIT 33.

Application of Cause & Effect Diagram

Meetings Take too Long – C&E Diagram

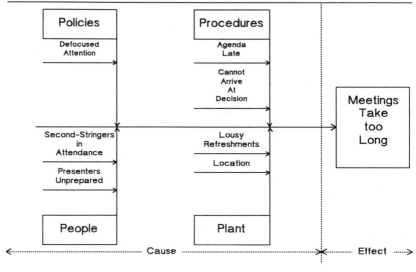

© MORE, Inc., 1990

with user-friendly, ''pop-up'' screens that aid in construction of both the table and subsequent C&E diagrams. In addition, after being transferred to Pareto Chart format, this table becomes a simple check sheet to aid in gathering data.

Exhibit 34 shows an example of a Pareto Chart. It provides a simple means to graphically portray data and assist PAT members in prioritizing alternatives. In this case, a show of hands provided a quantified measure for all the possible causes for the meeting taking too long. The data, or show of hands, are logged onto the check sheet, input into the computer, and graphed to produce the results you see in Exhibit 34. The tallest column, to the left of the graph, shows how time might be spent overcoming the predominant cause brainstormed during a C&E diagramming session. The results are graphic, easy to understand, and formatted suitably for presentation in open forum, or as documentation of a data analysis function in the PAT report. The Pareto Chart is very utilitarian in nature.

114

EXHIBIT 34.

Application of Pareto Chart

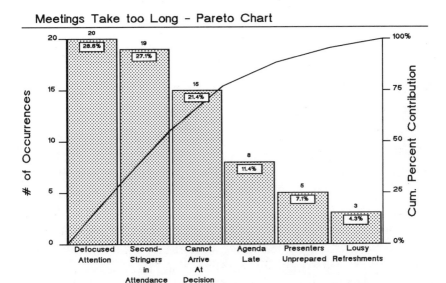

Meetings Take too Long – Pareto Chart

Beyond the simple C&E diagram and Pareto Chart described above, the MORE package offers many other capabilities that ease administrative and presentation burdens of PAT members. These include histograms, run charts, control charts, flow charts, and others. MORE has an excellent reputation for producing very reliable and usable products. For information on their package, "The Tools of Total Quality Management," contact:

> Technical Management Consortium, Inc.
> Terry L. Cook, Associate
> P.O. Box 13591
> Albuquerque, NM 87192-3591
> (505) 299-3983

Professional Affiliations for Assistance

The question often arises, "Where do I go for information on Total Quality?" At several points throughout this book, I have discussed the use of consultants and suggested several sources for training and consulting support. But what information outlets exist for the TQM Coordinator, the in-house consultant, or the company facilitator? I recommend three sources of information: The American Society for Quality Control (ASQC), The Association for Quality and Participation (AQP) and the Institute for Industrial Engineers (IIE).

The ASQC offers a monthly magazine, *Quality Progress*. Technical libraries usually have *Quality Progress* on their shelves. If you thumb through several issues, you'll find an abundance of relevant information for the quality professional on topics ranging from corporate strategy for improving quality, to the specific use of tools for measuring and improving processes. When first introduced to *Quality Progress*, I copied articles from the library edition so I could read them at my leisure. I realized that I was copying so much information that I joined the ASQC—just to receive the magazine. *Quality Progress* is a must for every quality professional. For more information about the ASQC, contact:

> American Society for Quality Control
> 11709 W. Dixon St.
> West Allis, WI 53214
> (800) 248-1946

Be sure to request a copy of their most recent book catalog. They undoubtedly will have one or two available for your specific circumstance, whether in finance, health care, or heavy industrial manufacturing.

The Association for Quality and Participation (AQP), a 7,500-member non-profit professional association, is an excellent resource for information about quality and participative management. AQP publishes a bi-monthly newsletter and a magazine, The Journal for Quality and Participation. Contributors to The Journal have included Joseph Juran, Phil Crosby, Elizabeth Dole, Armand Feigenbaum and Tom Peters. The Journal has also featured special issues for aerospace, health care, communications, government and labor.

AQP sponsors three annual conferences. A typical conference session might showcase NASA's benchmarking techniques, or detail how to implement high-performance compensation systems. AQP also carries over 150 titles of books, audio, software packages and video programs. AQP members have access to a research center with a lending library, and a 78-chapter and regional network spanning the U.S. and Canada. For more information about the AQP, contact:

> Association for Quality and Participation
> 801-B W. 8th Street, Suite 501
> Cincinnati, OH 45203
> (513) 381-1959

I also like the *IIE Monthly Magazine*, an invaluable source for the quality professional. Don't let the title mislead you—it is not just for engineers. I recently found an excellent article on how to quantify costs and benefits associated with hospital out-patient care, which I will use as an example in a workshop on quality in service organizations. This is not the type of material you would generally expect to see in professional engineering magazine. Their editing is good, the articles brief and to the point, and most important, they provide plenty of graphics for describing key concepts.

Another excellent article I read in *IIE Monthly Magazine* related to the use of an electronics spreadsheet as an aid in planning an office reorganization. It explained who should be located where, and how support equipment should be placed for most effective utilization. I like this example. Everyone goes through this sort of experience sooner or later. For more information about the Institute of Industrial Engineers, contact:

> Institute of Industrial Engineers
> 25 Technology Park/Atlanta
> P.O. Box 6150
> Norcross, GA 30091-6150
> (404) 449-0460

117

Chapter 8. Phase 4: Diversification

Congratulations, you have arrived! After preparation, planning, assessment, and implementation, you are finally ready to move onto the fifth, and final, phase of implementing TQM--Diversification. Here, you capitalize on your experience and success and begin to invite others into the improvement process. Logical candidates for invitation include subordinate organizations and suppliers. If your first PAT only touched a few of the functional areas within your corporation, diversification may consist of spreading the word through the rest of the organization. Exhibit 35 shows the steps necessary to accomplish Phase 4 successfully.

People often wonder, "Why wait so long to let everyone else know what's going on?" The answer is not all that straightforward, so I will address this question as we progress through this chapter.

Involving Others

The first step in diversification involves inviting subordinate organizations into your TQM improvement process. The Corporate Council provides a logical entry point for them. Here, senior managers view your organization and the function of the improvement process. Also, the TQM Coordinator briefs senior management on the benefits of TQM, based upon your own experiences. A walk-through of your organization, observing a PAT at work, and reviewing recent success stories can work wonders. Yes, share both

EXHIBIT 35.

Phase 4: Diversification

△ **Subordinate Organizations Brought into Improvement Process**

△ **Supplier's Brought into Improvement Process**

△ **"Suppliers Day"**

© Joseph R. Jablonski, 1990

the good news and the unexpected pitfalls you have encountered. The initial investment toward improvement should be made by the parent organization. A team consisting of the TQM Coordinator, a facilitator, and the organization CEO and/or President should plan to spend time at the subordinate's facility selling the concept of TQM and your experiences with it.

Alas, one of the greatest reasons for demonstrating success prior to involving others is because they will ask difficult questions. In fact, they will ask the same questions you, your managers, and your workforce personnel have had during the early stages of implementing TQM--questions like, "How do you know it can work for us?" or "How can you be sure management supports it?" I refer to these concerns as the "yeah buts." If people are reluctant to make the change, and most are, then the "yeah buts" creep in. They look for every excuse not to pursue the change toward total quality. People must feel they can benefit from this, or they will try to delay, discredit, or cancel the initiative. If you seek their support without first proving credibility within your own company, you are walking on shaky ground. I recommend you hold off. Wait until you establish credibility before expecting others to improve. If you still feel compelled to somehow involve a subordinate organization, include a senior representative from that organization in your Corporate Council. This way, he or she will feel a part of this important initiative from the highest level of involvement, gaining valuable experience in accommodating the successes and challenges of making change happen.

Bringing Suppliers on Board

This is a hot topic because no company can offer anything of quality to its clients without support from the providers of goods and services. What makes this subject particularly interesting is that companies moving toward TQM often reduce their number of suppliers significantly. In doing so, they tighten the bond between their remaining suppliers and themselves.

Shortly after introducing subordinate organizations to TQM, bring your suppliers, vendors and subcontractors on board. Invite everyone who sells you products or services. Tours of your organization, reviews of your Corporate Council at work, and briefings by senior management should set the tone. Suppliers will learn how they can benefit from what you have done, and how you both can realize savings and become more competitive in the marketplace. You're a team.

Supplier's Day

A "Supplier's Day" provides a convenient opportunity for initiating two-way communication between your organization and your supplier. Ask suppliers for feedback on what they have seen in your organization that may benefit them. More important, encourage them to identify how TQM may help them. Arrange provisions for one-on-one or small group working forums between your organization and supplier personnel to discuss specific applications of TQM. Some suppliers may be surprised to discover how the principles and tools of TQM have already been used successfully to improve the quality of their delivered products and services because of actions taken by earlier PATs.

Where Suppliers Go for Assistance

Your suppliers can use two primary sources for bringing TQM into their organization. The first is obvious--it's you. The second is from a consultant. If you are in the public sector the Federal Quality Institute (FQI) will provide services to you.

Yes, your suppliers will come to you first for information on TQM. "Supplier's Day" can prepare you for that first important supplier exposure to TQM. Here suppliers are sold on the concept as they see its results in action. Also, you will be expected to provide training for your suppliers' employees, at least for some of them. This occurs commonly. Earlier, when I discussed the successes of some quality greats, such as Milliken and Motorola, I mentioned they have a "Quality College" where they train their employees. They also train many of their suppliers' there as well.

The second source your suppliers can use is a consultant. As described in Chapter 5, a consultant offers specialized expertise and has a wealth of experience to draw upon as you implement change. Appendix A provides a list of consulting and training sources.

Another excellent source of information (for Federal Agencies) is the Federal Quality Institute (FQI). Within government, the FQI serves as the focal point and champion for Total Quality Management. Its Charter includes:

(1) Conduct Quality Awareness Seminars for Federal Government managers stressing the organizational requirements of a quality culture, a systematic approach to continuous improvement, a strong focus on the customer, employee involvement, and excellence in products and services to the public;

(2) Provide Federal agencies with a Federal Supply Schedule for a simplified method of obtaining professional assistance in implementing TQM; and

(3) Provide a clearinghouse for productivity and quality improvement information for the Federal sector through a Resource Center.

For more information on the services available to Federal agencies through the FQI, contact:

The Federal Quality Institute
Pension Building
Box 99
Washington, D.C. 20044-0099
(202) 376-3747

Chapter 9. Implementation Schedule

This chapter describes a realistic schedule for TQM implementation. It also reveals the interrelationship between Phases 0 through 4, as discussed in Chapters 4 through 8. Exhibit 36 summarizes these interrelationships and provides a top-level schedule.

As you can see in this exhibit, four specific things must occur for this five-phase implementation approach to work in a coordinated manner. Each is described below. Remember, in Phase 0 resources are committed only to accomplish planning, so the Corporate Council can intelligently decide on whether or not to proceed with full implementation.

(1) Initiation of Phase 1, Planning, occurs at the conclusion of Phase 0. The organization's Key Executives decide to proceed and approve funding to initiate the planning phase.

(2) Once the Corporate Council approves the TQM Implementation Plan and commits resources, Phase 3, Implementation, begins.

(3) When support services are on-line and available to offer consulting and specialized training to Process Action Teams, the first few teams can be chartered and given the go-ahead to proceed.

(4) The diversification effort should be planned, but not implemented, until the parent organization has realized its first success story.

Exhibit 36.

Schedule

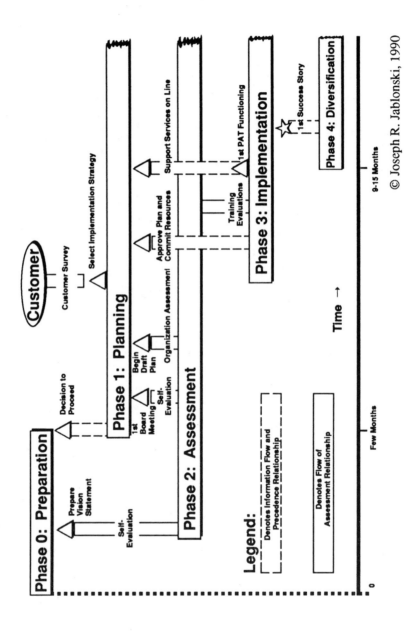

© Joseph R. Jablonski, 1990

Four specific assessment vehicles--self-evaluation, organizational assessment, customer surveys, and training evaluations must come into the TQM implementation process to make it successful. Although the precise timing of these surveys and questionnaires is not fixed, there are logical points where they can provide the most help and at the same time, not become administratively burdensome during the assessment phase. Each is described below.

(1) The first assessment involves a self-evaluation by the organization's key executives. This will probably occur during an off-site meeting, while developing the organization's vision statement. The self-evaluation at this particular time helps Key Executives answer some big questions such as, ''Why are we in business?'' ''What are our strengths?'' and ''Where can we improve?''

(2) Another self-evaluation is performed, this time by the Council members. Remember that the Key Executives discussed above now comprise part of the Corporate Council. This self-evaluation aids in understanding the organization's strengths and weaknesses. This exercise should result in a TQM Implementation Plan and council charter which build on the strength of the organization.

(3) An organizational assessment must be completed before the Corporate Council can begin preparing its Draft Implementation Plan. As described in Chapter 6, this assessment consists of two parts. First, an independent consultant completes a questionnaire during one-on-one interviews with a small sampling of the organization's employees. Second, a significant number of employees complete and submit individual questionnaires. In both cases an independent, third party compiles and analyzes the results. The results are presented to the Corporate Council as a guide for addressing specific needs within the organization while preparing the TQM Implementation Plan.

(4) Training evaluations are collected after each training session involving executive, management, and workforce personnel and submitted to the training department for analysis. The training department and the TQM Coordinator review the results of this analysis as a means of refining similar training sessions in the future. These results are also presented to the council members, reassuring them their money is being well spent.

127

(5) Last is the customer survey. This information should be gathered before the council's decision to select an implementation strategy. The TQM Coordinator compiles these surveys and analyzes them to assess the organization's strengths and weaknesses and then presents the results to the council. Again, these results will be maintained by the TQM Coordinator and a trend analysis performed after gathering each additional set of data.

The bottom of Exhibit 36 indicates that Phase 0 can be accomplished within a few months. You can reasonably expect your first success story within six months to one year from the time Phase 1, Planning, begins.

Chapter 10. Estimating Implementation Resources

This section explains three methods used to ''price out'' the resources necessary for implementing TQM. It concludes with a suggested approach you might use to estimate the personnel and financial resources necessary to implement TQM in your organization. The three methods described will give you an appreciation of those factors that are routinely accounted for in estimating. More important, they will identify factors that are frequently overlooked.

The three types of cost estimates reviewed here include:

(1) Percentage of Workforce

(2) Man-Hours per Employee

(3) Bottoms-up Training Estimate.

Each is described below.

The American Quality and Productivity Center estimates that about 1.25 percent of the total organization workforce, in terms of man-years, is directly attributed to the role of implementing TQM. This staffing figure seems reasonable. Assuming a total workforce of 300 persons and a fully-loaded rate of $150k per man-year, we see that TQM implementation under this approach will equal $562k per year. We can also assume that the expenditure of staffing resources will be apportioned between in-house and hired consultants and trainers. The details of this calculation are included in Appendix B.

The man-hours per employee estimate was developed from expenditures by the Naval Shipyard Pearl Harbor and adjusted to account for differences in workforce population and a fully-loaded man-hour rate. It's much easier to obtain this information from a public sector organization than from a private company. With this technique it is estimated $671k is necessary to implement TQM per year. It assumes a normalized workforce of 300 persons and $150k per man-year, fully loaded. This figure includes training, outside consulting support and meeting time for Process Action Teams to coordinate their efforts. Appendix C provides the details of these calculations.

I developed the third type, the bottoms-up training estimate. As the name implies, it ascertains the costs of training the workforce, based upon a set of assumptions. On-site and off-site training, travel, per diem, and time away from the job are included in this estimate. Appendix D provides the details of these calculations, which yield a total training cost of $616k per year. Like the estimates above, it assumes a workforce of 300 persons and a fully-loaded man-year rate of $150k. One factor which makes this estimate unique is its accounting for time away from the job during training. This cost must be accounted for as a cost to implement TQM, or folded in the organizations overhead rate. Also, this estimate includes one person per year for in-house training.

Exhibit 37 summarizes these results. Based upon these calculations, I suggest the following resource estimates for a 300-person organization.

TQM Staffing = 3.75 persons (1.25 percent of total workforce with one person-year per year dedicated to in-house training. Staffing includes the TQM Coordinator, consultants and trainers. (Please note that the consultants and trainers in support services include both in-house and contracted personnel.)

Training Resources should account for on-site training materials, facilities, off-site training, travel and per diem.

Time Away from Job for Training = $22k per year assuming thirteen-fourteenths of training time is results oriented training.

These figures might seem startling. Yes, they are substantial, but so are the savings. An economic analysis on the costs and savings realized by the Naval Shipyard Pearl Harbor to date indicates a return on investment in excess of 50 percent per year (Appendix E). This is a respectable figure not only for government, but for private industry as well. Moreover, this figure does not account for the cultural change beginning to take place within the organization. This change continues to yield dividends, as people begin to solve problems on their own. TQM does not cost--it pays.

EXHIBIT 37.

Estimated TQM Implementation Resources Based upon Various Types of Estimating Techniques

Type of Cost Estimate	Cost in K$/Year	Comment
Percentage of Workforce	562	Accounts for TQM staffing requirements. Unclear how training is included.
Man-Hours per Employee	671	Accounts for training, consulting, and PAT meeting time. Ignores time away from job for training.
Bottoms-up Training	616	Accounts for training, travel and training time away from job. Only partially accounts for TQM staffing.

Note: All estimates are based upon a total of 300 personnel. Calculations are included in Appendix B, C, and D.

Cutting Costs Without Sacrificing Quality

I recently conducted a workshop on Implementing TQM in Washington, DC. Mr. Richard Deichl, of ELDEC Power Conversion Division of Lynnwood, Washington, attended and through him, I learned much about their approach to implementing quality.

Power Conversion, a Division of ELDEC Corporation, has about 500 employees and manufactures custom-power supplies for aircraft and missiles. Their quality initiative began in early 1988 with the hiring of a Director of Corporate Quality with a proven record of success in the quality arena.

Since 1988, they have successfully initiated more than fifty continuous process improvements, some large and some small. Their ultimate goal is to create the spirit of continuous process improvement. Their efforts have proven worthwhile, as both large and small gains continue to cascade throughout the company. First, training was conducted for company executives and people who would later train everyone else in the company. Training at all levels consisted of an intense 16 hours of instruction. Topics included the Principles of Continuous Process Improvement, Measuring Quality Improvements, The Process of Quality Improvement, and Management's Role. Each employee completed the course with a three-inch, loose-leaf binder containing all of the information necessary to begin immediately improving company processes. What makes this effort unique is that Director- and Vice President-level personnel provide the training. The Quality Improvement Process (QIP) Coordinators continue to support the initiative by attending and facilitating selected team meetings and helping employees apply the training to routine process improvements. In addition, they encourage those participating in especially promising process improvement efforts to compete for "The ELDEC Quality Award," the company's own recognition for quality.

What impressed me most was their ability to accomplish equal or greater results than others by applying the appropriate amount of management commitment. The right people at the right levels provided training and direct employee support and encouragement.

Their reward is significant results with the expenditure of between one-half to one-quarter of what I've seen other companies spend.

ELDEC has initiated plans to apply for the Malcolm Baldrige National Quality Award. I think they are an excellent contender for our nation's most prestigious quality award and will represent America well. Good luck ELDEC.

Chapter 11. Concluding Remarks

TQM in Everyday Life

All around me I see continuous process improvement--I see TQM. As an officer in the Naval Reserves, I coordinate science fair judging at regional and state levels. Our purpose in this important effort is to encourage young people to pursue a technical profession after completing high school.

I recently judged a science fair in Las Vegas, New Mexico, at the Highlands University Wilson PE Complex. I evaluated a project prepared by a young man, a high school senior, named Chris. Chris demonstrated a simulator he had built to create and understand the phenomenon of hurricanes. What made this particular project notable was that it was his third and last year for participating in this event. As Chris described the details of his project, the numerous improvements he had made over the years became evident. These improvements resulted from his own learning. He had achieved them by tinkering, following up on helpful pointers from friends and teachers, incorporating feedback from encouraging science fair judges, and most of all, working hard. Improvements over the years, feedback, and hard work maintained his love for his project and gave him the encouragement to pursue his scientific interest upon completing high school. Chris already practices TQM and should serve as a good example to us all.

Closing

During a recent conversation, a friend of mine asked, "How can you spend so much time training, speaking, writing, and managing your business? When is there time left for Joe?" That's easy. First, I am fortunate to have a very supportive family. My wife, Pat, and sons, Joey and Michael, are behind me one hundred percent. My other advantage is an enthusiasm that allows me to pursue this important work. Though I have had the feeling for quite awhile, the words to describe it only came to light a few years ago.

At that time I was traveling to Wright-Patterson Air Force Base. After a long day, I decided to visit the Officer's Club for a beer. If you have ever seen the Officer's Club at Wright Pat, you will probably remember the gigantic, elegant brick structure. There are a lot of General Officers in the area, and where there is a lot of rank, there probably is an equally prestigious O-Club nearby. Anyway, I was sitting at a table chatting with an Air Force Reserve Officer who was assigned there for two weeks. I immediately noticed something special about this person. He had a very demanding, responsible job in his civilian career, yet somehow found time to fulfill his military reserve obligation. As he spoke, I began to understand his motivation. He spoke of his ground crew, their professionalism, the long hours of preparation before each flight, and the huge responsibility that accompanies flying a $15 million aircraft for the U.S. Air Force. He explained how he missed his family and why he maintained this grueling schedule. He said that during this two-week period each year, he spent a few precious hours in the air working with true professionals, who wanted to see him succeed at what he did best and then return safely to the base. He explained all the details of his most recent flight, only part of which I understood. He closed by saying, "I can't believe they pay me to do what I love."

When things get tough for me, I think of people like Paul at the University of New Mexico. He is presently completing his Masters Degree and will soon begin working on his Ph.D. He recently stopped me in the hall and told me that he had taken my training on white-collar applications of flow charts. He had used it in a presentation to an existing client, who checked off the boxes he wanted to sponsor in the near future. The illustration provided a clear picture of how they would achieve incremental improvements in their capabilities, allowing them to focus on the long-term final product. He thanked me for helping him get more business, in exchange for a few hours of his time.

The Lima Army Tank plant sent several representatives to one of my workshops only five months ago. They recently called and said they saved an estimated $150,000 in consulting fees by using my approach to implementing TQM—the very same approach you have just read about in this book. War stories and all! I maintain my interest and enthusiasm by knowing that someone I speak to today will someday return with a success story of his own. I find this a tremendously satisfying business. I enjoy helping individuals and companies do their jobs better, remain competitive, and improve their quality of work life. "I can't believe they pay me to do what I love."

If you have any ideas or experiences you would like to share with me on this important subject, please write to me directly at:

> Joseph R. Jablonski
> 2004 White Cloud NE
> Albuquerque, NM 87112

Thank you for reading my book. Best of luck.

Sincerely,

Joseph R. Jablonski

Appendix A

Sources of TQM Training and Information

Technical Management Consortium, Inc.
Attn: Mr. Joseph R. Jablonski, President
P.O. Box 13591
Albuquerque, NM 87192-3591   (505) 299-3983   FAX (505) 299-5788
Training, Speaking, Audio & Video Tapes, Consulting, TQM Software

Productivity Services, Inc.
Attn: Mr. Edward S. Roth, P.E.
3505 Camino Aplauso, NW
Albuquerque, NM 87107 (505) 344-7060
TQM Training in Simultaneous Engineering, Design for Producibility, and
Engineering Database for SPC.

MORE, Inc.
Stephen S. McCampbell, President
421 Montano NE, Suite A
Albuquerque, NM 87107 (505) 344-1233
TQM Software -- "The Tools of Total Quality Management"
Other Applications Programs for Professionals

Appendix B

Calculation of Percentage of Workforce Cost Estimate

Assumptions: Size of total workforce = 300 persons.
Cost for one man-year = $150k fully loaded.

Calculation based on percentage of total workforce times percentage of workforce dedicated to TQM staff at the labor rate mentioned above.

Therefore, total cost per year is:

(300 persons) (.0125) ($150K/man-year) = $562k/year

Figure of 1.25 percent obtained from American Quality and Productivity Center estimate, Houston, TX.

Appendix C

Calculation of Man-Hours per Employee Cost Estimate

Assumptions: Size of total workforce = 300 persons.
Cost for one man-year = $150k fully loaded.

Calculation #1: Determine the number of man-hours per person-year dedicated to TQM as a cost-determination scaling factor.

Total cost for training, PAT meetings and consultants over first three years of implementation = $1.8 + 7.8 + 8.6 = $18.2M. Source: *Total Quality Management (TQM) at Pearl Harbor Naval Shipyard,* A Top-Level Planning Document, Date and Author Unknown, 20 pages.

Total shipyard workforce = 6000 persons with 60% of workforce trained during three year period. Loaded labor rate = $55/man-hour. All figures per telephone conversation with G. Damon, TQM Office, Pearl Harbor Naval Shipyard.

Number of trained persons during first three years =
(6000 persons)(0.6) = 3600 persons

Total dollars for TQM per person, per year =
($18,200,000)/(3 years)(3600 persons) = $1685/person-year

Therefore, cost per person, per year in terms of man-hours is:
($1685/person-year)/($55/man-hour) = 31 man-hours/person-year

Calculation #2: Determine TQM costs per assumptions and results above:

(31 man-hours/person-year)(300 persons)($150k/man-year)
* (1 man-year/2080 man-hours) = $671k/year

Appendix D

Calculation of Bottoms-Up Training Workforce Cost Estimate

Assumptions: Size of total workforce = 300 persons.

Distribution of total workforce:

Executive	9	persons
Management	90	persons
Workforce	201	persons

Training estimates in days per person in each category:

Executive	4.5 baseline training
Management	3.5 baseline training
Workforce	2.0 baseline training
	4.0 extended training

All travel days rounded up to next integer for costing purposes.
Costs for off-site training = $300/day.
Per Diem = $150/person-day. (Travel days rounded up for costing purposes)
Travel = $450/trip.
Cost for one man-year   =$150k fully loaded
                         = $72/hour.
Training days available = 250/year

1. Calculate Executive Training Costs:
Off-site training costs:
    (9 persons)(4.5 days)($300/day) = $12.2k

Travel and per diem costs:
    (9 persons){($150/person-day)(5.0days/person)+$450/trip} = $10.8k

Time away from job costs:
    (9 persons)(5 days/person)(8 Hours/day)($72/hour) = $25.9K

2. Calculate Management Training Costs:
Off-site training costs:
    (90 persons)(1.5 days)($300/day) = 40.5k

On-site training costs:
    (90 persons)(2 days/person)(8 hours/day)($72/hour) = $103.7k

Total training cost = $40.5k + 103.7 = $144.2k

Travel and per diem costs:
    (90 persons){($150/person-day)(2.0 days/person)+$450/trip} = $67.5k

Time away from job costs:
    (90 persons)(4 days/person)(8 hours/day)($72/hour) = $207.4k

Appendix D (Cont.)

Calculation of Bottoms-Up Training Workforce Cost Estimate

3. Calculate Workforce Training Costs:

Off-site training costs:
(201 persons)(4 days/person)($300/day) = $241.2k

On-site training costs:
(201 persons)(2 days/person)(8 hours/day)($72/hour) = $231.6k

Total workforce training cost = $241.2 + $231.6k = $472.8k

Travel and per diem costs:
(201 persons){($150/day)(4 days)+$450/trip} = $211.0k

Time away from job:
(201 persons)(6 days/person)(8 hours/day)($72/hour) = $694.7k

4. Estimate On-Site Training Persons:

Total on-site training days = (9 persons)(4.5 days) + (90 persons)
(3.5 days) + (201 persons)(2 days) = 758 training days

Total estimated on-site training persons:
(758 training days)/(250 days/person-year)/(3 years) = 1 person/year

Summary of Results

Category	No. of Persons	Baseline Training Recomm.	Extended Training Recomm.	Training Cost(k$)	Travel and Per Diem (k$)	Time Away From Job (k$)
Executive	9	4.5 days	-	12.2	10.8	25.9
Management	90	3.5	-	144.2	67.5	207.4
Workforce	201	2.0	4.0 days	472.8	211.0	694.7
Totals	**300**			**629.2**	**289.3**	**928.0**

Total of all costs for 3 years = $1,846k
Total of all costs for 1 year = $616k

Appendix E

Calculation of Rate of Return for Naval Shipyard Pearl Harbor

Year	TQM Costs	TQM Savings
1986	$1.8M	$10.8
1987	7.8	5.6
1988	8.6	7.6

Source of information: ***Total Quality Management (TQM) at Pearl Harbor Naval Shipyard,*** A Top Level Planning Document, Date and Author Unknown, 20 pages.

Cash Flow Summary:

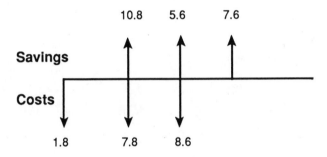

Calculate Rate of Return per Year:

P = -1.8 + 3.0(S/P,i,1) - 3.0(S/P,i,2) +7.6(S/P,i,3)

A zero solution for P was sought by substituting values of S/P for various interest rates from ***Cost and Optimization Engineering,*** by F.C. Jelen and J.H. Black, Published by McGraw-Hill, Inc., New York, NY, 1983.

Result: Annual Rate of Return > 50%.

Bibliography

Alexander, R.S., Colonel, USAF. "Total Quality Management - The ASD Experience." Aeronautical Systems Division ASD/CCT, Wright-Patterson AFB, OH.

Cooke, R.A. and D.M. Rousseau. "Behavioral Norms and Expectations: A Quantitative Approach to the Assessment of Organizational Culture." Group & Organization Studies. 13, 245-273, 1988.

Cooke, R.A. and J.C. Lafferty. Organizational Culture Inventory. Plymouth, MI: Human Synergistics, Inc., 1989.

Cooke, R.A. (ed.) Organizational Culture Inventory Leader's Guide. Plymouth, MI: Human Synergistics, Inc., 1989.

Crosby, P.B. Quality Without Tears: The Art of Hassle-Free Management. New York, NY: McGraw-Hill Book Company, 1984.

Damon, G.A. "Implementation of Total Quality Management at Pearl Harbor Naval Shipyard." Journal of Ship Production. Vol. 4, No. 2, May 1988.

DiPrimio, A. Quality Assurance in Service Organizations. Radnor, PA: Chilton Book Company, 1987.

Drucker, P.F. Management Tasks, Responsibilities and Practices. New York, NY: Harper & Row, 1974.

Girard, J. with S.H. Brown. How to Sell Anything to Anybody. New York, NY: Warner Books, 1979.

Hansen, Richard L., Capt., USAF. An Overview to the Application of Total Quality Management. Aeronautical Systems Division ASD/CCT, Wright-Patterson AFB, OH.

Iacocca, L. with W. Novak. Iacocca: An Autobiography. New York, NY: Bantam Books, Inc., 1984.

Jaueh, L.R. and J.B. Townsend. Cases in Strategic Management and Business Policy. New York, NY: McGraw-Hill Book Company, 1986.

Lorange, P. Implementation of Strategic Planning. Englewood Cliffs, NJ: Prentice Hall.

Mackay H., Beware the Naked Man Who Offers You His Shirt. New York, NY: William Morrow and Company, Inc., 1990.

Miller, J.C. III (Signatory). Quality Improvement Prototype, Internal Revenue Service-Federal Tax Deposit System - Department of the Treasury. Office of Management and Budget.

National Institute of Standards and Technology. "1990 Application Guidelines: Malcolm Baldrige National Quality Award."

Ohmae, O. The Mind of the Strategist - Business Planning for the Competitive Advantage. New York, NY: McGraw-Hill, Inc., 1982.

Phillips, D.T. et al. "SEMATECH: IE at Work in the Trenches to Meet Worldwide Competition." Industrial Engineer Magazine. Dec. 1989.

Schonberger, R.J. Japanese Manufacturing Techniques: Nine Hidden Lessons in Simplicity. New York, NY: The Free Press, 1982.

Schonberger, R.J. World Class Manufacturing: The Lessons of Simplicity Applied. New York, NY: The Free Press, 1986.

Stratton, B. "Xerox and Milliken Receive Malcolm Baldrige National Quality Awards." Quality Press Magazine. Plains, IL, 1989.

Total Quality Management: Designing and Managing the Process. Seminar Proceedings, Produced and Distributed by the American Productivity and Quality Center, Houston, TX, 1989.

Walton, M., with Foreword by W.E. Deming. The Deming Management Method. New York, NY: Dodd, Mead & Company, 1986.

Glossary

Benchmarking - (1) A technique to evaluate your performance in specific areas when compared to recognized leaders. You may be comparing yourself to competitors or similar processes and functions at other geographic locations within your own organization. (2) A technique to establish a baseline for the existing performance of a process in the organization which subsequent measurements could be compared against to identify trends.

Brainstorming - A technique used to generate numerous ideas using the composite talent and experience of a group in a facilitated meeting environment.

Cause & Effect Diagram - A graphic technique for summarizing the results of a brainstorming session, identifying the causes of a specified undesirable outcome. Also referred to as "Fishbone Diagrams" and "Ishikawa Diagrams" (after their developer, Professor Kaoru Ishikawa of Tokyo University).

Control Chart - A graphic technique for identifying whether an operation or process is in or out of control and tracking the performance of that operation or process against calculated control and warning limits.

Corporate Council - The corporate entity responsible for chartering Process Action Teams, committing corporate resources, removing barriers to process improvement, and participating actively in the TQM initiative. The Corporate Council includes the organization's Chief Executive Officer/President and top representatives from each of the organization's functional areas (ie. Marketing, Operations, Administration, etc.).

Executive - A member of the top two levels on the organizational chart. Those individuals responsible for the strategic course of the organization, generally consisting of the CEO/President, deputies, and functional managers. Functional managers may be Vice-Presidents, Directors, etc.

Facilitator - An individual with excellent communication and interpersonal skills who conducts organized meetings and encourages the group to arrive at a consensus on issues involving the members of the group.

Flow Chart - A graphic technique using symbols to identify the operations involved in a process, their interrelationships, inputs, and outputs. A basic tool of TQM, flow charting routinely comprises the first step in understanding selected processes in an organization.

Key Executives - A small portion of all corporate executives who are routinely consulted first on important issues confronting the organization.

Management - Individuals who supervise the workforce directly or indirectly and/or manage individual projects and are responsible for accomplishing short-term organization objectives.

Management Commitment - A commitment of corporate resources, including executive and manager time, to the Total Quality improvement process.

Pareto Diagram - A graphic technique that uses data to help PAT members identify where scarce resources should be applied to reap the greatest gains. It helps to prioritize options, portraying the results as a bar diagram.

Process - A series of operations or activities linked together to provide a result that has increased value.

Process Action Team (PAT) - A group of 4 to 8 members that applies the principles and tools of TQM to (1) identify opportunities for process improvement, (2) understand existing processes and identify where the greatest gains can be realized from process improvement, (3) provide recommendations for process improvement, and (4) implement process improvement.

Quality - Those attributes of a product or service that the customer attaches value to. Depending on the customer's focus, ''Quality'' may include surface finish, timeliness, size, cost, reliability or other factors.

Total Quality Management (TQM) - A cooperative form of doing business that relies on the talents and capabilities of both labor and management to continually improve quality and productivity using teams.

TQM Coordinator - That individual charged with the overall responsibility of ensuring that the "mechanics" of implementing TQM are carried out. He/she serves as a trainer, facilitator, coordinator, and organizer of TQM-related resources, and maintains statistics on the progress of Total Quality. Geographically close to the CEO/President on the corporate organizational chart, the TQM Coordinator is consulted on issues related to the corporate quality initiative and serves as the Secretariat to the CEO/President during Corporate Council meetings.

Workforce - Those individuals responsible for accomplishing the day-to-day activities of the organization, interacting with customers, and creating the impressions necessary to form and cement positive customer attitudes toward the company.

Index

150

Order Form

Three Ways to Order

1. Call:

(505) 299-3983

2. FAX to:

(505) 299-5788

3. Mail to:

Technical Management Consortium, Inc.

P.O. Box 13591

Albuquerque, New Mexico 87192-3591

Name: _____

Title: _____

Company: _____

Address: _____

City: _____ State ____ Zip _____

Telephone: (____) _____

( )_____ **Book:** Implementing Total Quality Management: Competing in the 1990s ISBN 1-878821-00-8 $17.95 each

( )_____ **Audio Cassette:** Implementing Total Quality Management: Competing in the 1990s ISBN 1-878821-01-6 $19.95 each (90 minutes, 45 each side)

( )_____ **Six-Cassette Audio Series:** Implementing Total Quality Management: Competing in the 1990s ISBN 1-878821-05-9 $99.95 (40 minutes each cassette)

( )_____ **Workbook:** Implementing Total Quality Management $25.00 (32 pages)

( )_____ **Computer Software:** The Tools of Total Quality Management $495.00

Add $5.00 Postage & Handling for Each Order

New Mexico Residents Add 5.75% Gross Receipts Tax

Method of Payment

( ) Full Payment Enclosed - Make check or P.O. payable to: Technical Management Consortium, Inc.

( ) MasterCard

( ) Visa

Card Number: _____

Expiration Date: _____

Signature: _____

( ) Please send me information on the Consulting, Product, and Training Services available through Technical Management Consortium, Inc.

153